RTPI

mediation of space · making of place

from design policy to design quality

The treatment of design in community strategies, local development frameworks and action plans

Matthew Carmona
John Punter
David Chapman

UCL
Bartlett School
of Planning

CARDIFF
UNIVERSITY

PRIFYSGOL
CAERDYⱠD

Published by Thomas Telford Publishing, Thomas Telford Ltd,
1 Heron Quay, London E14 4JD.
URL: http://www.thomastelford.com

Distributors for Thomas Telford books are
USA: ASCE Press, 1801 Alexander Bell Drive, Reston, VA 20191-4400, USA
Japan: Maruzen Co. Ltd, Book Department, 3–10 Nihonbashi 2-chome, Chuo-ku, Tokyo 103
Australia: DA Books and Journals, 648 Whitehorse Road, Mitcham 3132, Victoria

First published 2002

A catalogue record for this book is available from the British Library

ISBN: 0 7277 3194 7

Typeset by Kneath Associates, Swansea
Printed and bound in Great Britain by Latimer Trend, Plymouth

Authors

Matthew Carmona is at the Bartlett School of Planning, University College London, email: m.carmona@ucl.ac.uk

John Punter is at the Department of City and Regional Planning, Cardiff University, email: punterj@cardiff.ac.uk

David Chapman was formerly at the Bartlett School of Planning, University College London, email: dchapman@Koetterkim.com

Acknowledgements

The authors would like to thank the following people:

Robert Upton for all his help in bringing this work to publication.

Kevin Murray and Meredith Evans who as, respectively, Chairs of the Urban Design Working Group and Urban Design Panel at the RTPI have given the project their valued support.

Peter Ellis from the Office of the Deputy Prime Minister (ODPM) for his valuable comments on an earlier draft.

All those at the RTPI who commented on the many drafts including Bob Chalk and David Jarman, and in particular, the members and Secretariat of the Urban Design Panel:

Kenny Brown   Jeremy Caulton
Colin Haylock   Emily Lauder
Mike Lowndes   Eileen Thomas
Loise Waring

The Economic and Social Research Council and Department of the Environment (as they were) for funding the original research.

James Murphy at Thomas Telford Publishing for his help and patience.

Last, but by no means least, all the local authorities and planning officers who supplied extracts, gave interviews, and commented on the recommendations in the early drafts of the guide, in particular:

- Sarah Johnston and Simon De Beer, Bath & North East Somerset Council
- David Carter and Douglas Lee, Birmingham City Council
- Rohan Torkildsen, Bristol City Council
- Archie Onslow, London Borough of Camden
- Bob Wills, Cheltenham Borough Council
- Elfed Roberts and Chris Vickery, Cotswold District Council
- Matthew Evans, Guildford Borough Council
- Eleanor Thom, London Borough of Haringey
- Peter Vaughan, Leeds City Council
- Ian Tomie and Kathy Cooper, Leicester City Council
- Hilary Jordan, Purbeck District Council
- Jenny Pearce, London Borough of Richmond
- Peter Rainford, Sheffield City Council
- Karl Kropf and Andy Wharton, Stratford on Avon District Council
- Barry Sellers and Zbig Blonski, London Borough of Wandsworth
- Rosemarie A. MacQueen, Westminster City Council

Contents

Chapters

Insets

Figures

Foreword

Local planning authorities have a lot on their plate. Over-stretched and under-resourced, they are responding to many challenging Government agendas including planning reform, best value performance indicators and community strategies.

In testing circumstances, there is a tendency for authorities to focus on getting the planning process right, with perhaps less time spent on ensuring the quality of development on the ground.

This guidance document from the Royal Town Planning Institute (RTPI) aims to bring product and process together, by demonstrating a variety of tools and methods for embedding a commitment to well-designed buildings and spaces within plan-making and decision-making processes.

The Commission for Architecture and the Built Environment (CABE) works with many planning authorities across England and there is great variation in the ways in which planning authorities tackle design issues. Some authorities have dedicated urban design teams or officers, some use design advisory panels. Some authorities make significant use of Supplementary Planning Guidance to capture design policies, others focus on the quality of individual site briefs.

As the many case studies in this guide illustrate, there is no one-size-fits-all solution. The needs of urban and rural authorities will differ. Different approaches will also be required in areas of high and low development demand.

There are, however, some common requirements. Every authority needs a clear set of design policies that have authority and a clear means of implementation. Every authority needs access to design skills to help members and officers make design judgements. And every authority needs to be championing the importance of design to prospective developers by establishing clear benchmarks of the standard of quality that is expected.

Design is a competitive good. It is those authorities that prioritise the quality of the built environment that will increasingly attract and retain business occupiers, households and visitors. For this reason alone, this guide merits serious consideration.

Jon Rouse
Chief Executive
CABE

1

A framework for design policies

A framework for design policies

The purpose of this guide

It is the objective of this guide to offer each local planning authority in the United Kingdom a framework for the development of a comprehensive range of design policies. These are seen as a necessary underpinning for all planning interventions within the built environment. In the wake of the 2000 Urban White Paper, the 2001 Planning Green Paper, the formation of the inter-professional Urban Design Alliance (UDAL), and the increasingly influential work of the Commission for Architecture and the Built Environment (CABE), this is an appropriate moment to reconsider the role of design policies within planning practice. This is especially so given the proposals in the 2002 *Planning Policy Statement (PPS): Sustainable Communities – Delivering through Planning* to replace the current system of development plans with a new generation of community strategies, local development frameworks and action plans embracing what was formerly a wide range of supplementary design guidance.

The key recommendations build on those outlined by the Department for Transport, Local Government and the Regions (DTLR) and the CABE in *By Design Urban Design in the Planning System: Towards Better Practice* (2000), the most recent advice on how to improve the practice of urban design in the planning system, and which relates to urban, suburban and rural contexts alike. Twenty key recommendations are made under four headings that are brought together in **Inset 1**.

The structure of the guide

The guide follows a simple eight-part structure. Following this introduction, the role and purpose of design policies are discussed and the key recommendations contained within this guide are placed within the context of other recent initiatives to improve the design dimension of planning.

The next four chapters form the heart of the guide and consider in turn the position of, and priorities for, design within policy frameworks, the fundamentals of design policy writing, the key aspects of design policy which require coverage (moving from strategic to more detailed scales of operation), and key issues concerned with the implementation of design policies.

The final two chapters discuss (briefly) other influences on design quality and how the writing and implementation of design policies fits within a wider agenda for delivering better designed development, and concludes by offering a range of documentary sources that offer further advice. Wherever possible, relevant case study material has been used to illustrate the key recommendations, while a wide range of up-to-date policy extracts have been included to demonstrate best practice.

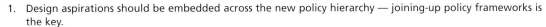

Inset 1: Summary of recommendations

The process of design policy writing

1. Design aspirations should be embedded across the new policy hierarchy — joining-up policy frameworks is the key.

2. As well as being a focus of dedicated policy in its own right, the pursuit of design and environmental quality should infuse all other policy areas.

3. Utilise previous implementation experience in policy writing — policy writing and development control must work in partnership.

4. Design policies can emphasise key stages in the control process, such as application presentation, consultation and design briefing.

5. Analytical area appraisals should underpin policy formulation and be informed by public consultation.

The fundamentals of design policy

6. Design policy represents an opportunity to establish a positive vision and agenda for future change across the authority's area.

7. Ensure that development responds appropriately to its context — visual, social, functional and environmental — as a fundamental policy objective.

8. Policies should be based on a broad concept of urban design that integrates built and natural environment concerns — sustainability is a fundamental design objective.

9. Authorities should develop a clear spatial design strategy at authority-wide and area-wide scales that should be related to their key strategic objectives.

Key aspects of design policy coverage

10. Urban design policies embracing townscape, urban form, public realm, mixed use and layout, and movement considerations should be the cornerstone of design policies.

11. Considerations of landscape should pervade policies at all scales of design and will be a critical element of sustainable development.

12. Policies should encourage the use of architectural skills and the development of contemporary designs that respect their surroundings.

13. Policies should encourage the coordination and positive management of the urban environment.

14. Design criteria for conservation policies should be derived from conservation area assessments that emphasise design opportunities as well as constraints.

15. Policies should encourage the preservation of listed buildings and pay special attention to the qualities identified in their listing, and to their settings.

Writing, implementing and monitoring design policies

16. Policies should specifically respond to the most commonly encountered design problems and application inadequacies.

17. Policies should be written with the means of implementation in mind — design consideration type policies are the most useful form of expression to achieve this.

18. Area and site-specific guidance should be organised hierarchically, cross-referenced to authority-wide design policy, and preferably be adopted in the local development framework.

19. Design policies should be systematically implemented through appropriately skilled development control processes that allow adequate time for negotiation.

20. Design policies should be systematically monitored to assess and improve their effectiveness, and to ensure political and public support for design control.

The research

The guidance presented here derives from four sources. First, in 1993, the authors undertook a research project for the then Department of the Environment (DoE), subsequently published as a research report *Design Policies in Local Plans* in 1996. Second, this work was extended and refined in a study funded by the Economic and Social Research Council (ESRC) between 1994 and 1995 and published as *The Design Dimension of Planning* in 1997 (Punter and Carmona, 1997).

Third, the recommendations of the aforementioned studies were condensed into a draft Royal Town Planning Institute (RTPI) Planning Practice Standard and in 2000 an extensive consultation exercise was undertaken involving over 50 local planning authorities (chosen to reflect different development contexts from around the UK), and the RTPI, DTLR and UDAL. Finally, the work was updated in 2001/2002, in the light of impending developments in planning policy and practice, and a new country-wide trawl for best practice in policy writing was completed.

The recommendations have also been informed by the range of related research initiatives undertaken by the authors between 1995 and 2001 (see Chapter 8). In total, therefore, the recommendations have developed out of the authors' research extending over a period of almost ten years.

The scope and limitations of the guide

The research on which this advice is based focused on the development of design policy in England. For this reason references to Government guidance are all to English guidance. Nevertheless, guidance issued in Scotland, for example in NPPG1: The Planning System and *Designing Places, A Policy Document for Scotland* (Scottish Executive, 2001); in Wales in Planning Guidance (Wales): Planning Policy and TAN(W)12: Design; and in Northern Ireland in PPS1: General Principles and in *Creating Places, Achieving Quality in Residential Developments* (DoE (NI), 2000). All offer similar support for both the analysis and recommendations, and the authors consider that the approach advanced in this guide is appropriate for all local planning authorities across the UK.

The work draws on local planning authorities' experience of writing design policies for development plans over the last 12 years, but it relates its recommendations to the new forms of statutory planning strategies, frameworks and action plans that will be required in the future. The recommendations are very deliberately focused on the policy dimension of design. In this regard they complement other initiatives emanating from other bodies discussed in the text. The intention is to ensure that the best practice evident in a few local planning authorities up to now is adopted by the majority in the future.

Writing a guide on design policies and planning at this juncture has been rather like trying to hit a moving target. This is because the planning system itself, and the role of planning policy in particular, is undergoing significant change. Thus in England, the 2001 Planning Green Paper — *Planning: Delivering a Fundamental*

Inset 2: Key provisions in the 2001 Planning Green Paper and *Sustainable Communities* Planning Policy Statement (PPS) with regard to design policy

The 2001 Planning Green Paper effectively proposed recasting the development planning process. The proposals reacted to a number of perceived weaknesses with the planning system:

1. Planning, and, in particular, the multi-layered hierarchy of adopted plans, is too complex.
2. The process is too slow, with plans often out of date before they are adopted.
3. Planning is too often negative and seen as a set of rules aimed at stopping development, rather than encouraging high quality development.
4. Policy frameworks often lack clarity and therefore undermine the predictability of the process.
5. The system fails to engage the interest of the communities for whom it is operated.

The need for and value of the planning system is emphasised. But the plan-led system should be based on a simplified policy hierarchy; shorter, better focused plans that can be adopted and revised more quickly; better integration between planning policy and other local strategies; more community involvement in policy preparation; and a system that delivers better quality development.

Key provisions, including those modified in the 2002 Planning Policy Statement *Sustainable Communities — Delivering Through Planning*, included the following.

Replacing development plans (structure plans, local plans and unitary development plans) with local development frameworks constituted of:

- a 'core strategy' consisting of a statement of core policies setting out the local authority's vision and strategy to be applied in promoting and controlling development throughout the area;
- more detailed 'area action plans' for smaller local areas of change, such as urban extensions, town centres and neighbourhoods undergoing renewal, or for areas of conservation;
- a 'proposals section' setting out site-specific policies outside of area action plans. The proposals section should contain a proposals map setting out key designation, i.e. conservation areas, sites for particular land uses or where particular policies apply, and locations for existing or proposed area action plans;

- non-statutory guidance such as a design statement for a particular authority-wide topic, or less formal area action plans or site development briefs.

That the core strategy would be short, focused and strategic in nature consisting of:

- a written statement of core policies for delivering the spatial strategy and vision for the area;
- a reasoned justification;
- mainly criteria-based, and location, rather than site-specific policies;
- a key diagram;
- a 'Statement of Community Involvement' setting out arrangements for involving the community in the continuing review of the framework, and in significant development control decisions.

That area action plans would articulate a clear physical vision for their areas, would have a strong design emphasis, and would provide a basis for community engagement. The Planning Green Paper defined four types:

- area master plans — comprehensive plans for a major area of renewal or development covering design, layout and location of new houses and commercial development supported by a detailed implementation programme;
- neighbourhood and village plans — setting out how the distinctive character of a neighbourhood, village or parish is to be protected, the location of any new development, the key services and facilities, and the design standards to be applied;
- design statements for particular areas— setting out the design standards and related performance criteria for the area;
- site development briefs — setting out detailed guidance on how a particular site is to be developed.

Change — presaged a root and branch review of the plan-making process. It, and the later *Sustainable Communities* PPS, confirmed, however, that the plan-led system will remain the cornerstone of the UK planning system, while the pursuit of design quality will continue to increase in significance (**Inset 2**).

With regard to design, four key principles underpin the new planning agenda:

1. The pursuit of design quality is a major planning objective.
2. The pursuit of environmental quality and more sustainable forms of development represent overarching concerns that should infuse all parts of the planning remit.
3. Development plans are to be streamlined, both as regards the processes leading to their adoption and their length — they will become Local Development Frameworks (LDFs).
4. Local development frameworks will include more detailed policy instruments in the form of action plans that will embrace the key elements of supplementary design guidance.

By adopting the recommendations outlined in this advice, authorities will be able to move beyond partial, ad hoc and inconsistent approaches to design policy, towards more considered, comprehensive and character-based approaches based upon professional and public consensus. The recommendations will help to provide clear policies that can underpin the local authority's corporate policy making, its direct interventions into the physical fabric and, of course, all of its planning and development control activities. They will help ensure that quality design is no longer viewed as an optional extra.

2

The design dimension of planning

The design dimension of planning

The Government commitment

Recently there have been calls in many governmental and professional quarters for more sophisticated approaches to the handling of design concerns as part of the planning process. PPG1: General Policy and Principles suggests that urban design, building design, and landscape design are all matters of proper public interest (paras 13–14), while PPG3 confirms that 'local planning authorities should reject poor design, particularly where their decisions are supported by clear plan policies and adopted supplementary design guidance' (para. 63).

Since 1994, a cross-party consensus has gradually emerged on the need for more effective consideration of design in planning. In December 1997, in a Ministerial speech, the key message of PPG1 was emphasised, that 'good design should be the aim of all those involved in the development process' and that 'design policies should be set out in development plans, against which development proposals should be judged, thereby giving greater certainty to all those involved'. As Central Government recognises in PPG1 (para. 15), design policies can help to underpin the promotion of sustainable development, environmental quality, and social and economic regeneration. Indeed, along with sustainable development, design has a particular status as an 'underpinning theme' of the Government's approach to the planning system (para. 3). This status is confirmed by the treatment of design across the range of PPGs as a concern that impacts on almost every other sector of planning interest (**Inset 3**).

More recently this position has been confirmed in the Urban White Paper. Speaking in December 2000, the Minister argued: 'Government's commitment to better urban design is not a passing fad. On the contrary, it is central to our crusade for quality'. Since then, research on *The Value of Urban Design*, published by the CABE and the Department for the Environment, Transport and the Regions (DETR) (2001) clearly established the 'value added' by better quality design. The work concluded that as well as social and environmental benefits, better urban design enhances investment returns and levers in economic dividends through more profitable and sustained regeneration activity. The same research confirmed that the role of urban design in positive planning was potentially decisive in delivering such value.

Current practice — moving on

Despite the research findings, until recently, design policies and control practices were rarely written down and systematised in local planning authorities, and policy writers and development controllers often failed to collaborate in policy writing. Policy writing was generally absorbed by osmosis from office practice, and design policies frequently gave a large measure of individual discretion to both planning officers and councillors. As a consequence, there has been a general failure to

Inset 3: Good design: a key objective of the planning process — what Government guidance says

PPS: *Sustainable Communities — Delivering Through Planning*
'Too often the culture of planning is reactive and defensive. We want a culture which promotes planning as a positive tool: a culture which grasps the opportunities…improving the process by which development adds value to communities through better design.'

PPG1: General Policy and Principles
'The appearance of proposed development and its relationship to its surroundings are…material considerations in determining planning applications and appeals. Such considerations relate to the design of buildings and to urban design.'

PPG3: Housing
'Good design and layout of new development can help to achieve the Government's objectives for making the best use of previously-developed land and improving the quality and attractiveness of residential areas. In seeking to achieve these objectives, local planning authorities and developers should think imaginatively about designs and layouts.'

PPG6: Town Centres and Retail Development
'Town centres must provide a high quality environment if they are to continue to be places where people wish to come. The Government wishes to promote greater consideration of design, particularly urban design, not least in order to help improve the environment in our town centres.'

PPG7: The Countryside — Environmental Quality and Economic and Social Development
'New building in rural areas should contribute to a sense of local identity and regional diversity, and be of an appropriate design and scale for its location…Good design helps to maintain or enhance local distinctiveness, and can help to make new development more acceptable to local people.'

PPG8: Telecommunications
'In seeking to arrive at the best solution for an individual site, authorities and operators should use sympathetic design and camouflage to minimise the impact of development on the environment.'

PPG13: Transport
'The physical form and qualities of a place, shape — and are shaped by — the way it is used and the way people and vehicles move through it. New development should help to create places that connect with each other sustainably…People should come before traffic. Places that work well are designed to be used safely and securely by all in the community.'

PPG15: Planning and the Historic Environment
'There has been increasing recognition in recent years that our experience of a historic area depends on much more than the quality of individual buildings — on the historic layout of property boundaries and thoroughfares; on a particular "mix" of uses; on characteristic materials; on appropriate scaling and detailing of contemporary buildings; on the quality of advertisements, shop fronts, street furniture and hard and soft surfaces; on vistas along streets and between buildings; and on the extent to which traffic intrudes and limits pedestrian use of spaces between buildings."

PPG17: Sport and Recreation
'Open space, whether or not there is public access to it, is…important for its contribution to the quality of urban life. It enhances the character of conservation areas, listed buildings and historic landscapes; it can attract business and tourism; it is part of the urban regeneration process.'

PPG19: Outdoor Advertisement Control
'The main purpose of the advertisement control system is to help everyone involved in the display of outdoor advertising to contribute positively to the appearance of an attractive and cared-for environment in cities, towns and the countryside.'

PPG21: Tourism
'Tourists visit historic towns not just for the big set pieces — the cathedrals, the castles, etc. — but for the wider experience of a historic environment with strong local character. So the total fabric of the town is very important — the lesser buildings as well as the greater, the details of surfaces and street furniture, and the spaces between buildings.'

PPG22: Renewable Energy
'The aim of the planning system is to secure economy, efficiency and amenity in the use of land in the public interest. Planning decisions have to reconcile the interests of development with the importance of conserving the environment.'

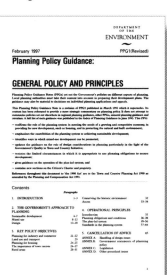

develop a full range of design policies, and evidence persists of a lack of confidence (and frequently competence) among authorities in their ability to secure good design (**Inset 4**).

In the context of today's plan-led system, such wide discretion is no longer desirable if the concern for good design is to move beyond the 'subjective' and 'idiosyncratic'. The revised guidance in PPG1 confirms this, stating: 'Where the design of proposed development is consistent with relevant design policies and supplementary design guidance, planning permission should not be refused on design grounds unless there are exceptional circumstances' (para. 19). This is an important statement because it establishes a contract between applicant and authority, and between officers and councillors. It suggests that applicants should take design considerations seriously if they expect to get planning permission but, equally, authorities should take the time to carefully formulate policies because once in place they will be expected to abide by them. In this way greater certainty will be offered by the planning process, and the delivery of a high standard of design will become the expectation rather than the subject of unnecessary tension and protracted negotiation.

In this regard, design — perhaps more than any other area of planning policy — needs to move beyond subjectivity, to more objective decision-making based on a clearly articulated policy framework and a set of design principles and criteria

Inset 4: Authority 'X' Policy H07 — what not to do!

All too often design policies have been based on little more than vague references to 'amenity', the need for new development to be 'in keeping' with existing development (whether that is good or bad), and that poorly specified design standards (usually space around dwellings and road layout standards) should be maintained. Authority 'X' only had one policy (H07) to influence the design of development. The resultant quality of development has been low!

DESIGN AND LAYOUT

H07 NEW RESIDENTIAL DEVELOPMENT SHOULD BE LAID OUT SO AS TO:

PROVIDE A HIGH QUALITY OF BUILT ENVIRONMENT WHICH IS IN KEEPING WITH ITS SURROUNDINGS.

INCORPORATE OPEN SPACE FOR BOTH FORMAL AND INFORMAL USE IN ACCORDANCE WITH POLICY RE6 OF THIS PLAN.

ENSURE THAT RESIDENTS OF THE NEW DWELLINGS WOULD HAVE A SATISFACTORY DEGREE OF PRIVACY AND AMENITY.

AVOID ANY UNACCEPTABLE EFFECT ON THE PRIVACY AND AMENITY OF THE OCCUPIERS OF NEARBY PROPERTIES.

PAY DUE REGARD TO EXISTING FEATURES AND GROUND LEVELS ON THE SITE.

SUBJECT TO THE ABOVE FACTORS, TO INCORPORATE FEATURES TO ASSIST IN CRIME PREVENTION.

Residential development is not only the homes and immediate living environment of its occupiers, but also constitutes part of the fabric of the local area. It is therefore essential that the new housing both provides good living conditions for those who live there and forms an attractive and well-integrated feature of the locality. It is also important, while taking into account the need for good overall design, to devise general layouts and detailed features aimed at enabling crime prevention.

Poor design policy to poor design quality

agreed by the community. Furthermore, it will be particularly important to clearly articulate these aspirations in the local development framework as this will be the document that carries statutory weight.

The role of design policies

This guide, like *By Design*, recognises that through the writing of a comprehensive (although not necessarily detailed) range of design policies, authorities are securing for themselves the most effective and resource efficient tool with which to influence design quality (**Inset 5**).

Inset 5: *By Design* — Government advice on design policies

By Design describes a four-part 'planning toolkit' for influencing urban design:

1. **Understanding the local context** — by appraising local context, identifying constraints and opportunities, and considering the national and regional policy context.
2. **The development plan** — from policy objectives to general and more specific policies.
3. **Supplementary design guidance** — including urban design frameworks, development briefs and design guides.
4. **Development control** — from pre-application negotiations, to processing the application and making a decision, to post-application monitoring.

The guidance argues that the adopted plan provides an essential framework for guiding and controlling development and should:

- provide the overall vision for the area;
- identify the main objectives to realise that vision;
- define the local context for people and places;
- set out the overall design policy framework against which the local authority will assess development proposals;
- provide the policy foundation for supplementary planning guidance.

By Design offers the following advice on design policies in development plans (pp. 42–46):

- **The plan should set out the sort of place the authority wishes to see** — both in terms of broad corporate objectives and as regards the physical form. It should actively establish a land-use strategy that meets these aims, for example by relating areas of growth to transport infrastructure.

- **Every plan should be different** — in order to reflect the unique circumstances of every place, which should be expressed in the design objectives adopted and how design policy is structured. In some plans it may be appropriate to structure the plan in terms of design objectives; in others it may be appropriate to focus on aspects of development form.
- **The plan should explain how its design vision has been shaped** — by national and regional policies and by an appraisal of context, for example.
- **Policies should interpret not repeat national policy** — by relating generic design objectives to the local context and sub-areas and to particular recurrent design issues.
- **Policies should be well written** — each policy should be clearly expressed and concise, and should include a clear design aim, the criteria against which planning applications will be considered, a reasoned justification (including cross-referencing to other policies) and a statement on implementation.
- **Different policy types are appropriate** — 'general design polices' need to establish a comprehensive policy framework for design across the plan area, and provide the basis for development control when no specific policies apply. 'Area-specific', 'site-specific' and 'topic-based' should relate to particular local conditions on the basis of rigorous appraisal of character, but only included if the issues are not adequately covered in the general design policy framework.

Design policies can, at one and the same time:

- outline an authority's design aspirations and vision for their area and emphasise the role of design in achieving it;
- embody the design aspirations of the local community (broadly defined);
- create scope for the appropriate, objective and consistent consideration of design issues through the development control process;
- offer designers useful guidance, and developers and the community increased certainty about acceptable design outcomes;
- guide the 'process' of design as well as the outcomes to ensure appropriate consideration of site, context and sustainability considerations alongside community concerns;
- establish an integrated framework for all forms of design policy and guidance; and, perhaps of greatest significance
- offer the foundation for a more positive, enabling and even visionary planning process that delivers better quality development.

Although most development plans are now in place, it is hoped that the timing of this guide will encourage the development of more effective approaches to securing good design as local development frameworks are written for the first time. As well as its primary role in providing guidance for those planning authorities engaged in design policy writing, this guide should also be of value in setting a broad design agenda for practitioners in both public and private sectors engaged in the preparation of other forms of design advice. Many of the recommendations may also be relevant to the range of other plans and strategies that local authorities are required to prepare, including local transport plans and neighbourhood renewal strategies.

What follows, therefore, is a comprehensive agenda for design policy writing that not only embraces a broader conception of urban design than has hitherto been adopted in most practice, but also takes on board concerns about sustainable development.

The resources required

The recommendations in this guide are conceived very much as an 'ideal'. It is recognised that some of the recommendations require an increased allocation of staff time and resources before they can be implemented, particularly notions of area appraisal, thoroughgoing design consultation or ideas about the consistent monitoring of policies. Nonetheless, these are the kind of fundamental issues that require careful consideration, experimentation and collaboration with a wide range of constituencies over the long term if design policies are to be greatly improved and strengthened.

Most recommendations require little or no extra staff resources beyond the officer time to think through a new set of policy considerations and apply them to the locality. Most of the recommendations therefore are achievable over a short-term time horizon and can be implemented as authorities reconsider their policies in the light of the new planning arrangements.

3

The process of design policy writing

The process of design policy writing

The role of design in policy

First, it is possible to state some general recommendations about the quality and utility of design policies, and about the way in which their refinement should proceed.

The first two recommendations concern the local planning authority's priorities as regards design policy and the position of design policies within the wider policy hierarchy. These issues are important because they make clear the position taken about the quality of design that will be expected within the authority. By emphasising the importance of design within the work of the planning authority at large, a powerful message can be sent to all departments within the local authority as well as to councillors. The same message will also be sent to an external audience of applicants for planning permission, local residents and other consultees, that design quality is considered a serious and significant policy concern.

1. Design aspirations should be embedded across the new policy hierarchy — joining-up policy frameworks is the key

With the impending replacement of structure plans, local plans and unitary development plans by local development frameworks, the policy hierarchy has changed. In addition, local authorities have a new duty under the 2000 Local Government Act to prepare 'Community Strategies' to promote the economic, social and environmental well-being of their areas and to contribute to the achievement of sustainable development. Government guidance on the preparation of community strategies clarifies that they must allow local communities to articulate their aspirations, needs and priorities, and coordinate the actions of the council, and of the public, private, voluntary and community organisations that operate locally. In other words, community strategies now have a role at the centre of local authority activities in articulating the vision of the authority and its community, and all its constituent services (**Inset 6**).

This central role was recognised in the 2001 Planning Green Paper and in the *Sustainable Communities* PPS, which both affirmed the role to be played by the new community strategies in informing the preparation of local development frameworks. In turn, the proposed local development frameworks will assist the delivery of the community strategy. The new design policy hierarchy is therefore rooted within the community strategy, but elaborated within the statement of core policies contained in the local development framework 'core strategy'. This will in turn inform policy in any action plans. The recommendations in this

Inset 6: The role of community strategies

Salford have pre-empted government advice, and have had a community strategy in place for over ten years. During that time the strategy has evolved to become the key departure point for policy making within the city. In 2001 a new 'Community Plan' was published, establishing the policy direction for the city for the next five years. The UDP, which was adopted in 1995, is now being rolled forward and will build on the broad vision outlined in the Community Plan. To ensure this happens, nine area plans are being prepared to respond to the views of the nine area community committees involved in drawing up the Community Plan. These area plans will have the status of supplementary planning guidance and will provide the detailed context for the Unitary Development Plan (UDP).

Salford's vision is to:

> 'create a city where people choose to live and work. We aim to improve the quality of life of all our citizens by creating an economically prosperous city with a buoyant and competitive economy; creating and maintaining strong, safe, healthy and sustainable communities where all citizens can participate to the fullest extent in decisions which affect their communities; providing a better education for all, to enable children and young people to thrive and fulfil their potential; creating a city that is good to live in by providing quality homes and a clean and healthy environment.'

Seven cross-cutting themes are established to deliver the vision, with the UDP having a particular role in creating 'a city that's good to live in'. Recent success in economic and cultural development in Salford Quays is increasingly put down to the high quality environment that is being delivered, and the more recent emphasis on design innovation. The drive for quality is to become a key theme in future policy development

Salford Community Plan: strategic themes and delivery

Salford, The Lowry, Salford Quays

guidance document relate to the three levels in this new policy hierarchy and refine them by adding a fourth (**Figure 1**).

With the 'slimmer and swifter' agenda now informing the production of policy frameworks (**Inset 7**), opportunities for authorities to define a set of authority-wide design policies should not be lost. In recent years, those authorities that have been most successful in delivering better designed environments have defined a strong and robust design agenda in their development plan, which is then detailed through urban design strategies, frameworks and development briefs at sub-area and site-specific scales.

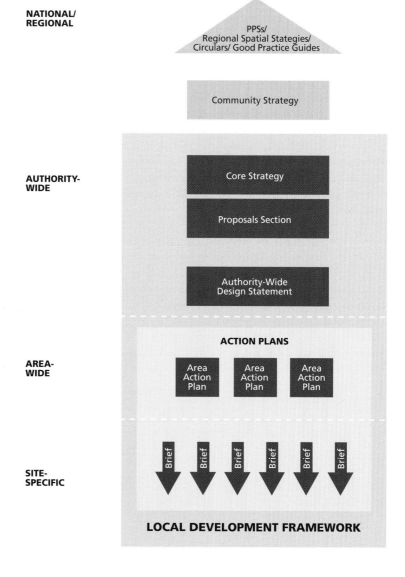

Figure 1: The new design policy hierarchy

Inset 7: Meeting the slimming down agenda

Both the London Boroughs of **Wandsworth** and **Richmond** were concerned that the use of 'design jargon' (and accompanying definitions) acted to increase the length of design policy. To avoid this, Richmond adopted the principles outlined in *By Design* on the basis that explanations and justifications would not be necessary. The borough simply provides bullet point criteria-based policy on key design issues and leaves *By Design* to fill in the gaps. This approach is also being taken forward in the borough's development briefs. Alternatively, Wandsworth plan to use illustrations as one means to reduce design policy explanation, while still expanding on and explaining policy. The council prefer to use illustrations instead of a glossary of terms and argue that it reduces overall policy length. This approach is also adopted in their supplementary design guidance.

Birmingham, **Bristol** and **Sheffield** anticipated that the drive for shorter and clearer plans would place more reliance on supplementary design guidance. They see the benefits being a less rigorous adoption procedure coupled with flexibility in producing additional design guidance as and when required. But the approach also removes the statutory status of much policy. Birmingham and Sheffield envisage this will result in the plan being more strategic with more detailed matters being dealt with elsewhere (an approach they have been using for some time because of the complexity of policy in their respective cities).

Birmingham, in particular, adopted the strategy of shorter and clearer plans several years ago.

Bath and Northeast Somerset and **Cheltenham** intend to remove policies little used by Development Control and Council Action policies (see **Inset 37**) as a means of reducing plan size without compromising utility. **Leicester** sees further opportunities to reduce plan size by consolidating policies, although this approach is not going to be used on design policies, in part reflecting their increased emphasis. **Cotswold** intends to reduce the number of proposal maps (see **Inset 17**), while **Guildford** is investigating the pros and cons of using more generic (less specific) policies.

Attempts to slim down plans have not always been straightforward. The **City of Westminster's** initial Deposit, Unitary Development Plan (2000) wholeheartedly took onboard Government advice to reduce the size of the plan, with, for example, every policy in 'Chapter 10: Urban Design' stripped down to a bare minimum. The move provoked criticisms from many groups, including the Royal Institute of British Architects (RIBA) and English Heritage for removing too much of the detail and justification. Westminster agreed in part with these responses and a second deposit plan reinstated much of the detail with the size of the urban design and conservation sections increasing dramatically to 59 pages.

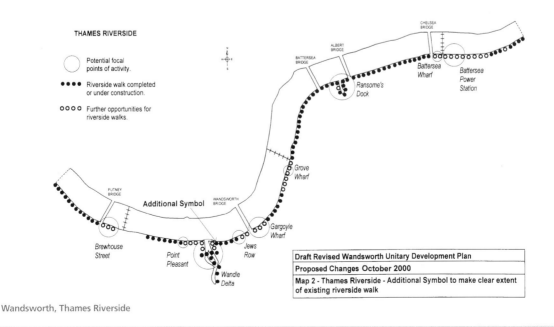

Wandsworth, Thames Riverside

Because of the expanding nature of the design agenda (Chapter 5), these policy frameworks in the development plan have become increasingly detailed and therefore incompatible with the requirement for streamlined plans (Leicester, for example, has 19 design-specific policies in its most recent development plan extending over 17 pages — **Inset 8**). The great value of setting out such comprehensive authority-wide design policy frameworks in the adopted plan has been:

- the statutory weight they possess in the development control process;
- their ability to act as a coordinating framework for other forms of guidance at an area-wide or site-specific scale;
- their relatively succinct coverage of the design agenda; and
- their ability to ensure that the quality of development is prioritised throughout the locality (not just in those places where more detailed guidance has been prepared).

Inset 8: A comprehensive policy agenda

Leicester has one of the most sophisticated and comprehensive approaches to urban design in its plan. The importance of design is established by addressing urban design in chapter three after the introduction and strategic themes. Placing it at the vanguard of the plan is a clear indication to applicants of the importance of design, and highlights urban design as an overarching concern of relevance across all types of development. The policies themselves range from issues of 'local setting and context' to 'waste disposal' and are supplemented by three tiers of further design guidance:

- city wide design guidance addresses specific design issues and provides additional generic information, detail and explanation across the city;
- area-based design strategies look at specific parts of the city, with a more detailed design framework produced for each;
- site briefs form the final level of design guidance and deal with specific development opportunities.

The draft status of the plan means that Leicester's urban design policies have — so far — not been tested at appeal (the

previous plan was not nearly so comprehensive). In the future, the council aims to reproduce the urban design chapter as a stand-alone guide, with extensive illustrations. The intention is to provide a more user-friendly and visually pleasing document. In the meantime the authority expects to streamline the urban design section following a request by the local plan inspector. Leicester's policy framework is implemented by the city's 25 strong multidisciplinary urban design section — one of the largest in Britain. The success of the team is reflected in the Bede Island North and South development. At Bede Island South, for example, the planning department negotiated an increased housing density, from 400–500 dwellings per hectare to 700, allowing a more urban proposal to be created by the developer.

Leicester, Bede Island

Local planning authorities need to retain an overarching and comprehensive design policy strategy at the authority-wide scale in order to deliver the better quality environments that central Government are increasingly seeking. Authorities are therefore recommended to produce an 'authority-wide design statement' as part of the local development framework. This would elaborate the core strategy and proposals section in the local development framework, and would inform the subsequent, more locally based action plans. It would ensure that design is prioritised everywhere (not just in areas where area action plans exist), while freeing up the core strategy from the necessity of presenting in detail a comprehensive design policy agenda. Explicit support for the preparation of generic authority-wide design statements as part of the local development framework was included in *Making the System Work Better* (2002; para. 24) issued by the Office of the Deputy Prime Minister (ODPM) alongside the *Sustainable Communities* PPS.

Inset 9 clarifies which of the recommendations in this guide relate to the different layers in the hierarchy.

- *Community strategy*. Because the community strategy establishes the corporate vision for the authority, it is important to establish within it a broad environmental and design quality agenda, as well as key objectives and targets for its delivery. This will subsequently apply across local authority services, including planning, highways, housing, economic development and

Inset 9: Key recommendations — relevance across the policy hierarchy

Recommendation (see Inset 1)	Community strategies	LDF core strategy and proposals section	LDF authority-wide design statement	LDF area action plans
1	✓	✓	✓	✓
2	✓	✓	✗	✗
3	✗	✓	✓	✓
4	✗	✓	✓	✓
5	✓	✓	✓	✓
6	✓	✓	✓	✓
7	✓	✓	✓	✓
8	✓	✓	✓	✓
9	✗	✓	✓	✓
10	✗	✗	✓	✓
11	✗	✗	✓	✓
12	✗	✗	✓	✓
13	✓	✗	✓	✓
14	✗	✗	✓	✓
15	✗	✗	✓	✓
16	✗	✗	✓	✓
17	✓	✓	✓	✓
18	✗	✗	✗	✓
19	✗	✓	✓	✓
20	✓	✓	✓	✓

urban and environmental management departments, and help emphasise design and environmental quality as core themes.

- *LDF core strategy and proposals section*. The LDF incorporates the next three layers in the hierarchy. It should be viewed as a delivery tool, rather than as a regulatory device, to establish, spatially articulate, and prioritise the social, economic and environmental future of the authority, its sub-areas and key sites, and to establish the quality thresholds expected by the council and the criteria by which the grant of planning permission will be decided. The broad vision set out in the community strategy is initially interpreted in the particular context of planning in the core strategy of the LDF. This should cover the fundamentals of design policy (see Chapter 4), including the conceptualisation of design adopted, the need to base design proposals on a clear understanding of context, and the contribution of better design to achieving sustainable development objectives. A broad authority-wide, map-based spatial strategy with detailed proposals should also be prepared and adopted at this level.

- *LDF authority-wide design statement*. The fundamentals of design policy can be expanded upon in the authority-wide design statement that should take the form of a comprehensive yet concise statement of design objectives with associated policy to deliver them (see Chapter 5). The aim should be to articulate the generic principles and policy (rather than area-wide or site-specific policy) that will apply across the authority's area, and to indicate how the vision and fundamentals outlined in the community strategy and core strategy are to be delivered. These types of policies will relate most closely to the 'general design policies' described in *By Design* (see **Inset 5**).

- *LDF area action plans*. Finally, the authority-wide policy should be elaborated as regards design in the range of more detailed area action plans (area master plans, neighbourhood and village plans and area design statements, for example). The aim here should not be to repeat wholesale policy at the authority-wide scale, but to interpret it to the range of different contexts found in the locality, including areas for regeneration, major development, or conservation, and important opportunity sites. The policies found in these plans will relate most closely to the 'area, site and topic' related policies described in *By Design* (see **Inset 5**).

In developing this new policy hierarchy, policies will become progressively more detailed and specific as they move towards the action plan level. It is important, however, that the policy hierarchy maintains a consistent design agenda that aims to join-up key contributions to design and environmental quality both from within and outside of planning practice. This should not imply mere repetition of policy, but instead a development and application of the key principles to the different objectives of each policy document: to meeting broad community objectives and the achievement of sustainable development in the case of community strategies; to articulating a vision for promoting and controlling development in the case of the core strategy; to the specifics of design in the authority-wide design statement; and to the planning needs of local areas and specific development opportunities in area action plans.

The recommendations that follow should be read with this first overarching recommendation in mind.

2. As well as being a focus of dedicated policy in its own right, the pursuit of design and environmental quality should infuse all other policy areas

In its more restricted meaning, design is just one of the range of considerations that local authorities need to consider. Nevertheless, if the broader view of design is taken as the creative manipulation of the built and natural environment, then design is central to planning and the achievement of a more visionary, quality-based agenda. This should be reflected in the location of design policies within policy frameworks.

Government guidance clearly sees design as a fundamental planning concern that infuses much of its guidance (see **Insets 2** and **3**). This approach can usefully be taken by authorities when structuring their own planning policy. Thus design concerns should first appear in the strategy or vision sections of the policy framework; core design issues should then be covered alongside conservation policies in a dedicated design or built environment section; and detailed, subject-specific concerns should infuse the remainder of the document as and when topics like town centres and retail development, transport and infrastructure, housing, or the rural environment are covered (**Inset 10**).

By such means it should be possible to:

- include a comprehensive coverage of design concerns without unduly lengthening policy documents — particularly the core strategy in the local development framework — so helping to keep plans quick and easy to read and understand;
- ensure that design quality is considered consistently across different types of development or localities; and
- ensure (through good cross-referencing) that the full design agenda is obvious to all users of these planning documents (**Inset 11**).

3. Utilise previous implementation experience in policy writing — policy writing and development control must work in partnership

A fundamental factor for the utility of design policies will be the quality of dialogue between design policy writers and the development controllers who have to operate the policies. The necessity of getting an extensive range of authority-wide policies written and adopted without delay has meant that in many authorities the input into policy from those charged with its implementation has sometimes been quite limited. As a result, development controllers are frequently suspicious about the basis of policies and have doubts about their overall objectives and practicality.

Inset 10: Design policy — indicative coverage by sector

Policy sectors	Policy coverage
Design and conservation	■ See Sections 4 and 5 and **Inset 31**

In addition to the issues identified in the built environment section of the plan, a range of specific design concerns should infuse the remainder of the plan to ensure design quality is considered in relation to all policy areas. Such concerns apply over and above those issues already included in design/conservation-specific policy. An indicative range of such considerations is listed by policy area below.

Policy sectors	Policy coverage
The rural environment	■ Landscape character ■ Native species ■ Ecological diversity ■ Relation to topography ■ Design of agricultural buildings — bulk/colour/materials ■ Settlement capacity and viability ■ Building re-use ■ Urban fringe ■ Signage and advertising
Transport and infrastructure	■ Access and sustainability ■ Modal integration ■ Density and public transport accessibility ■ Road hierarchy, design and safety ■ Integration of above ground infrastructure with streetscape ■ Integration of below ground infrastructure with streetscape ■ Street clutter reduction ■ Design and integration of telecommunications equipment
Employment and the local economy	■ Sustainable urban regeneration — pursuing quality ■ Design/integration of parking ■ Access by public transport ■ Mixed use strategies ■ New public space, management and access ■ Involvement in managing the public realm ■ Design of industrial estates — bulk/colour/landscaping
Town centres and retail development	■ Design/integration/security of parking ■ Shopfronts, signage and advertising ■ Avoiding trends of privatising the public realm ■ Living in town centres and living over the shop ■ Dealing with large volume uses ■ Design of retail parks — parking/landscaping/architecture ■ Lighting and street furniture ■ Diversity and the evening economy ■ Safety and security
Housing	■ Intensification in established residential areas ■ Road and footpath design (reducing car dominance) ■ Parking standards and density ■ Traffic calming and homezones ■ Mixing uses and tenures ■ Landscape, private gardens and greenery ■ Privacy and residential amenity ■ Community aspirations/involvement ■ Access and connection
Sport, leisure and community facilities	■ Open space provision, access and standards ■ Open space network ■ Design/integration of recycling facilities ■ Designing to reduce vandalism ■ Civic pride and the design of public buildings

The development of effective design policies has to incorporate fully the controllers' perspectives, so ensuring common objectives and consistency of approach to design matters between forward planning and development control teams (see **Inset 17**). In authorities with an urban design and/or conservation team, these professionals should be fully involved in the process of design policy writing.

In both design policy writing and control, if skills are not available in-house, it may sometimes be necessary to call on external specialists (either design consultants or officers from another local authority) to advise on design concerns. *The Value of Urban Design* research has shown that this positive use of resources can offer returns many times that of the original investment. For everyday proposals that do not require specialist input, however, it is important that policies are clear and readily usable by development control staff.

Inset 11: Design infusing the plan

Design quality is a cross-cutting theme of the **Bristol** plan and a key planning objective for the city. As such, design issues are addressed throughout the plan alongside the main themes of sustainability and regeneration. Chapter four 'Built Environment' contains the majority of urban design policies. Further design matters are included in the 'Introduction', 'Management of the Environment', 'Movement', 'Shopping' and 'City Centre' chapters. Policy L3 (Leisure), for example, establishes that the city's network of Greenways for walking and cycling will be protected. Development that incorporates these routes will be expected to ensure that the routes are fully distinguished from roads, with appropriate design details at junctions to give priority to pedestrians and cyclists. Public art is addressed in the 'Leisure' chapter, and is intended to increase the value of existing townscape and open space throughout the city.

Purbeck also has design quality as a major theme in its plan. The traditional 'Built Environment' and 'Natural Environment' chapters are now replaced by an 'Ensuring Quality of Life' chapter,

which addresses both encouraging social interaction and enhancing the quality of people's surroundings. The plan uses extensive cross-referencing to highlight the relationship between design and other areas of policy. Policy MN25 'Advertisements in Chapter Five: Meeting Economic and Social Needs', for example, establishes that advertisements will be permitted provided that they are well related to the scale and character of the building and its setting. Site-specific policy for 'Monkey World', Policy SS46, states that development will be permitted provided that it is sufficiently landscaped to screen it from the surrounding countryside.

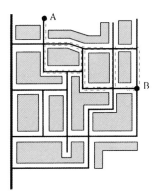

BRANCHED FORM OF STREET PATTERN
Permeability low
Only one route possible between A and B, and this route is not particularly direct

DEFORMED GRID LAYOUT
Permeability high
Choice of routes between A and B possible, and at least one of these routes is relatively direct

Purbeck, street patterns and permeability

Inset 12: The value of process policies

As part of their process-led approach to design, **Cheltenham** establishes the importance of the provision of adequate information on development proposals at the outset of their plan. The intention is to avoid misinterpretations and allow committee members to fully understand the submitted proposal. Process policies within the 'General Principles' section establish that, where appropriate, additional presentation material — including perspective drawings and models — may be required. Such policy confirms the importance of presentation and informs applicants of the requirements that may be placed upon them. The policies identify the scale and complexity of developments as the defining factor in determining the level of information required, and establish thresholds for their requirements in the policy justification. The policy justification also clarifies that schemes will be judged on a case by case basis.

The London Borough of **Richmond** adopts a similar approach in its criteria-based design policies. The intention is not to reduce design freedom, but rather to discourage submission of poorly considered and presented schemes. Policy BLT 11 'Design Considerations', for example, establishes that design standards represent a minimum prescription, and do not guarantee a successful scheme. Officers argue that it is difficult to know if this policy has impacted positively on the quality of submission because it

has been included in successive UDPs for such a long time. The authority nevertheless continues to be horrified by the general quality of schemes submitted, suggesting that BLT 11 may not yet be achieving its desired goal. Both Richmond and Cheltenham highlight the benefit of three-dimensional representation in applications. Richmond is even considering preparing its own computer-aided design (CAD) model of the built environment. The intention will be to insert proposed schemes into the model as they come forward.

Cheltenham GP1 Information to Accompany Planning Applications

Survey information

2.9 In order for the Council to determine planning applications properly and quickly, it is essential that developers provide full information at an early stage. Such information may be needed to set the development proposals in a broad context or for their implications to be assessed.

2.10 Relevant information will vary from site to site according to the site's size, location and character. The Council may consider any one or more of the items in Policy GP1 significant and will request such information to be submitted with a planning application or before it is determined (see also paragraphs 5.43–5.51 and Policies GE41, 42 and 43).

POLICY GP 1
INFORMATION TO ACCOMPANY PLANNING APPLICATIONS

Where appropriate, the Borough Council will require planning applications to be accompanied by:

(a) drawings showing the plans and elevations of adjoining and adjacent buildings, supplemented as appropriate by perspective drawings;

(b) a survey of trees and landscape features, such as ponds, hedges and significant wildlife habitats or corridors, covering not only the site but also adjacent or overhanging trees and other features;

(c) proposed service provision or drainage alterations which may affect trees and other features;

(d) measures to protect trees and landscape features during the construction process;

(e) a landscaping scheme showing details of proposed planting, paving and street furniture, as well as features to be retained;

(f) a wildlife habitat survey.

Richmond Upon Thames, new housing in Twickenham (Photo: Clive Chapman Architects)

4. Design policies can emphasise key stages in the control process such as application presentation, consultation and design briefing

An awareness of design as a process should underpin the whole approach to design policy writing and design control, but is particularly important in the formulation of detailed policy statements such as action plans. The 'process perspective' recognises design as a creative/analytical/cyclical thought process where a variety of contextual and development-specific considerations need to be weighed against one another, and where a variety of successful outcomes are possible. It also emphasises the many actors in the design process—clients, architect/designers, planners, politicians, the general public — and the need to recognise their different perspectives and inputs and relationships to one another.

Policy writing can beneficially reflect the process of design in the way in which policy is conceptualised and elaborated. In particular, it can establish a set of procedures, both formal and informal, for applicants and controllers to follow in developing and refining design solutions (**Inset 12**). For example, a process perspective, widely used by urban designers in current guidance, emphasises the various stages of design (**Figure 2**). It recognises that a key prerequisite of design quality is the creative skill of designers and their ability to respond to, or manipulate, the dual constraints of context and client aspirations. A process perspective therefore seeks to avoid dictating detailed design solutions. Finally, a process view provides for a set of explicit development control procedures that may be useful in encouraging good design:

- encouraging full analysis of the context and the site of proposed development;
- preparing development briefs and other action plans;
- making presentation requirements explicit (including the requirement in PPG1 para. A4 for a short written statement setting out the design principles adopted for an application);
- enabling pre-application consultation;
- monitoring the outcomes of design control processes on the ground.

A process perspective will be particularly important in the articulation of action plans, as a means to demonstrate how discussion on particular sites will be conducted and to outline processes of implementation.

Figure 2: The stages of the design and policy writing process

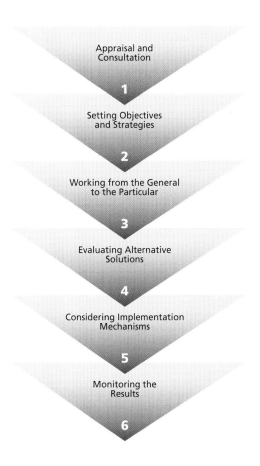

5. Analytical area appraisals should underpin policy formulation and be informed by public consultation

If ensuring that development respects its context is one of the key objectives of design policy, then a clear understanding of that context is critical. Appraisal of the character of the area or consultation with the affected public offer the means to achieve this. Ideally, area appraisal will include analysis of the natural world and this should become increasingly sophisticated over time, embracing not just topography, vegetation and landscape features but also the underlying natural processes of ecology and hydrology (see Chapter 4). Such appraisal should concentrate on protecting the most valuable resources and landscape character of a site in any development.

Area appraisal should also embrace the character of the built environment (**Inset 13**), including analysis of functional relationships, behaviour patterns and

Inset 13: **An approach to area appraisal**

The Borough of **Dacorum** is subject to considerable long-term pressures for growth. To overcome the problems associated with perceived town-cramming, it was decided to adopt the methodology devised by Tony Hall of Design Areas as a means to devise alternative policy approaches for different parts of each settlement. Thus, it was agreed to undertake a Residential Area Character Study (RACS) as a means to identify the areas of differing character that make up the residential areas of the borough's three towns. This could then be used to establish a locally responsive policy base against which planning applications for residential development could be reviewed.

It was anticipated that RACS would create an open, rational, locally determined and agreed statement on residential character, and a clear statement of the authority's commitment to design quality. Preparatory work began with the identification of 'character areas' in each of the towns by considering the physical qualities of each area and, subsequently, neighbourhood qualities, incorporating officer perceptions of sense of place. Survey work ensued using design criteria under four broad headings — housing, amenity, non-residential uses and traffic — each carefully defined and described in the resulting study.

The result was the definition of 74 character areas across the borough, each with a separate description and appraisal of character, followed by a statement of policy with additional elements covering the scope for residential development. The outcomes were considered during an extensive consultation exercise mounted on the RACS. The council approved the revised RACS in 1998 which was subsequently adopted as supplementary planning guidance. The character areas and policies were also included in the first revision of the Dacorum Borough Local Plan as a separately published but integral volume.

Dacorum, Hemel Hempstead residential character areas

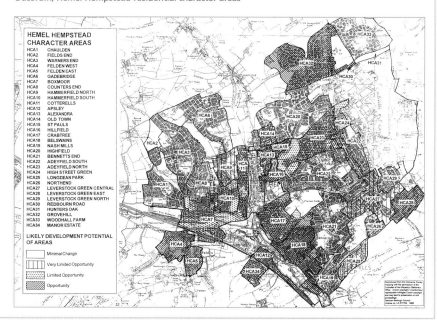

uses, urban grain, building-space relationships, three-dimensional forms, architectural character, the use of materials, townscape characteristics and historic and archaeological features. Fundamentally, however, appraisals should move beyond the mere descriptive, and should be written to explicitly identify positive and negative characteristics, as well as opportunities and constraints, and the principles for new development follow. Such analysis potentially provides the basis for widely shared, informed, consistent and objective judgements to be made about design priorities for the locality (**Inset 14**).

Despite the resource requirements of area appraisal, PPG1 emphasises both the importance of character assessment and the role of the public in the same (paras A1–A2); a message endorsed in the Urban White Paper. Appraisal seeks to define the key aspects of character which need to be conserved or changed and which need to be formulated into policy principles. It needs to be informed not just by

Inset 14: **Visual appraisal maps**

Purbeck utilise visual appraisal maps as an integral part of design policy for individual settlements. Each addresses a wide range of issues, such as landscape setting, edges, views, gateways, open space sequences, urban grain, heights, landmarks and so forth. They identify intrusive aspects, such as eyesores and the location of large-scale industrial buildings. Appraisals are included in the plan for all settlements with defined boundaries (25 in total), and are complemented by three written landscape appraisals in a plan appendix. The appraisals are produced in-house and each forms the basis for a settlement-specific design strategy with site-specific proposals. Appraisals are also used in conjunction with the council's general design policies to aid development control decisions.

Purbeck has included visual appraisals in the plan for over a decade. Officers nevertheless acknowledge that the appraisals could be moved to supplementary guidance, although at

present the authority has none (the plan covers all design issues). Officers argue that their current position allows design policies and settlement appraisals to be read as one. In the future, the settlement appraisals are to be replaced by conservation area appraisals again to be produced in-house. As Purbeck has no formal urban design section, the multidisciplinary planning team will undertake this work.

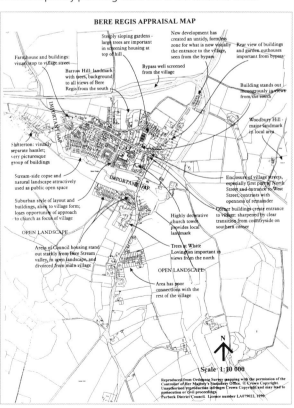

(Right) Purbeck, Bere Regis appraisal map

(Below) Purbeck, sensitive infill in Weighbridge

professional or scientific surveys but also by public consultation (and preferably genuine participation) in order to ensure that professional evaluations are supported by public preferences and community values. Communities might well be encouraged to conduct their own appraisals as a valuable way of collaborating in the design process (e.g. the Countryside Commission's work on Village Design Statements — **Inset 15**). Similarly, the wider public might participate in the monitoring process in feeding back views on the outcomes of the control process (see Chapter 6). Authorities are already required to produce a statement of community involvement as part of their LDF, a principle that might usefully be extended to appraisal work as well.

Significantly, the most comprehensive and useful area appraisals continue to be those produced for conservation areas, responding to the methodologies developed by English Heritage — approaches equally appropriate in non-

Inset 15: Involving communities in appraisal

In **Stratford-on-Avon** a number of approaches are in place that seek to ensure that policy tools are contextual and have community assent. A consultation exercise undertaken for the recently adopted *District Design Guide* (residential) was wide-ranging in its scope. 500 copies of the draft document were sent out to a list of consultees including most of the local housebuilders, the parish council, statutory bodies and appropriate consultees at a national scale. Housebuilders stated that as consultation was undertaken at a reasonably early stage, this enabled meaningful involvement and a positive outcome.

Stratford-on-Avon, the village of Kineton

Stratford promotes a full hierarchy of design guidance, including support and facilitation for Village Design Statements (VDS). VDSs are formulated through a community-led process, including community workshops and other techniques. A full-time project officer supports and enables the process. The community of Long Compton prepared a VDS as the residents were keen to maintain local character in the light of an increasing level of development pressure. A coordinating group was set up through the support of the Parish Council and with interested volunteers. The community-led process was undertaken with the help of the VDS project officer and step-by-step guidance material. The coordinating group produced the final document (over a year) through a process of questionnaires, participatory workshops and local consultation. The process was partly funded by the Warwickshire Rural Action Fund and the Parish Council, and was heavily reliant on volunteer time. Local people view the process and outcomes positively as providing an element of local 'control' and ownership of the process. The VDS operates as Supplementary Planning Guidance. Developers suggest that the VDS can increase levels of clarity in the planning process, but that issues of its interpretation by the local authority can still be problematic.

Stratford-on-Avon, Long Compton VDS

designated areas. The 'Placecheck' methodology has also been developed by UDAL as a means to comprehensively and systematically appraise localities, from the strategic down to the local and site-specific scales.

Clearly, some appraisal is better than none at all, and methodologies will need to be tailored to local circumstances and to the resources available for such work. A simple SWOT (strengths, weaknesses, opportunities and threats) analysis is therefore often the best and quickest place to start, perhaps placed against a framework of desired characteristics (**Inset 16**).

Appraisal should represent the fundamental basis for policy generation from the community strategy down to action plans.

Inset 16: A simple approach to appraisal

	Strengths	Weaknesses	Opportunities	Threats
Environmental capacity				
Townscape (visual composition of space)				
Urban form (three-dimensional built volume)				
Public realm (the social experience)				
Mixed use and tenure				
Connection and movement				
Landscape character				
Architectural character				

Instructions
1. Adopt a comprehensive urban design framework (in this case from Chapter 5 and Inset 31).
2. Combine with a basic SWOT (strengths, weaknesses, opportunities, threats) analysis.
3. Apply on a 'character area' basis, following a quick overview of the district in the field.
4. Record in written form and, where possible, in notational form on a map base.

Watch points

- **Learn from others.** A number of local authorities — large and small — have considerable experience in developing and writing urban design policies. Their experience can be used to avoid the potential pitfalls of writing design policy and to draw inspiration.

- **Avoid reinventing the wheel.** Much high quality guidance and literature on urban design is already available and quickly highlights the key aspects for consideration.

- **Avoid pattern-book approaches.** All principles need applying to the local context; there is little value in parroting Government guidance or other design conceptualisations without considering how they relate to the local context.

- **Consider the appropriateness of information.** Some design information is better placed outside core policy and in action plans and other supplementary guidance. Key themes should develop across the new policy hierarchy.

- **Embrace the 'slimmer and swifter' agenda.** The new policy hierarchy should not be seen as a threat to established policy frameworks, but as a way of better directing them towards desired audiences. The plan now needs to be viewed as a sequence of inter-linked policy documents and no longer as a one-size/style-fits-all document.

- **Speak to other specialists.** It is important that the implications of pursuing better design standards across other policy sectors (i.e. housing, transport, etc.) are discussed, understood and accepted by specialists in those fields also. Communication is the key!

- **Systematic appraisal takes time and resources.** It is nevertheless essential if policy is to be contextually relevant. Start with those areas under greatest pressure for change. The simplest appraisal is better than none.

- **Aspire for the best.** Environmentally, economically and socially disadvantaged areas if anything have even more right to aspire for the best quality development. Demanding high quality urban design costs no more to deliver and will not drive away investors.

- **Grab the opportunity.** Action plans provide the best opportunities to-date to create a positive and proactive urban design agenda. The opportunity should not be lost.

The fundamentals of design policy

4

The fundamentals of design policy

The developing agenda

It is now possible to turn to a set of fundamental recommendations on design policy and highlight those of greatest importance. These recommendations are based upon four inter-related observations (**Figure 3**).

- There is a need to recognise a tendency in development control (not necessarily confined to planners) to focus on design detail (especially elevations) and to miss more fundamental issues about the impact and appropriateness of development.
- Closely related to the first point, there is a need to rescue design control from an exclusive concern with individual developments and their visual relationships with their neighbours, and to inject a larger scale perspective on where development should go, what form it should take, and what its content should be.
- There is a need too to retain the social dimension of design, through greater consideration of public realm and the positive behaviour patterns that it can support.
- There is a need to address broader environmental issues that have introduced a sustainability agenda to urban design, notably landscape, ecology and hydrology.

Because of their fundamental nature, the recommendations in this chapter should be reflected in the LDF core strategy.

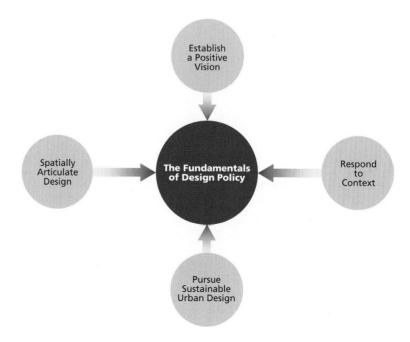

Figure 3: The fundamentals of design policy

6. Design policy represents an opportunity to establish a positive vision and agenda for future change across the authority's area

Much contemporary debate focuses around the potential of the planning system to be a positive instigator and manager of change, as opposed to a reactive responder to events. This relates to fundamental questions about the nature and purpose of planning which often come back to planning's loss of vision as one reason for its marginalisation in public policy (both locally and nationally). Increasingly it is being argued that planning needs to become a much more creative force for change, and use a positive engagement with design to articulate future urban forms that will capture public support.

The changes introduced through the Planning Green Paper clearly reflect this view, by emphasising a more positive and proactive — even visionary — role for local authorities in planning, not least in the requirements to prepare community strategies and long-term visions (spatial strategies) for their areas, as well as a range of action plans. In this regard design considerations should be embedded across the different scales of planning: within broad strategic aims; visions for particular areas of the policy framework (in separate action plans); and in the more detailed objectives to be applied at the local and development-specific scales (**Inset 17**). Design in this sense implies more than a concern for architectural, landscape or even urban design, it relates to a broader pursuit of quality inherent in all types of

---

Inset 17: **Design — strategic to local concerns**

Cotswold's design policies work from strategic to local concerns. The plan is organised in nine volumes with strategic design policies primarily located in the 'District-Wide Policies' and 'Proposals' section of volume one. Eight further volumes deal individually with each of the district's sub-areas. The latter provide village by village analysis, each with their own set of policies, some for specific sites. The approach was taken following a policy decision to produce statements for individual settlement, with each having an individual proposals map. These settlement-specific documents then refer back to volume one of the plan and its overarching design policies. The key aim has been to maintain local distinctiveness in design and to ensure that essential aspects of the 'Cotswold style' (see **Inset 35**) are embodied in new development. Guidance is also influenced by feedback on design policies from development control officers, including experience at appeal.

The plan was originally broken down into geographical areas because it was believed that a combined document would have been too unwieldy. This approach was also intended to reduce the cost of the plan to end-users. Future plans will nevertheless be reduced to two volumes in light of the Government's advice on producing shorter and clearer documents. The Cotswold intends to achieve this by reducing the number of proposal maps, with, for example, maps for each conservation area no longer being included. Officers do not, however, expect their approach to design to change, which they see as one of the strongest and most robust parts of the plan. Sustainability is however seen as a future cornerstone of policy.

Cotswold, reinterpreting the Cotswold style

environment and in all planning decisions. It relates to areas of particular historic sensitivity as well as to areas in need of large-scale development or regeneration, and to all types of context — urban, suburban and rural.

The community strategy and core strategy in the local development framework represent the appropriate vehicles through which to establish such a vision and to establish what sort of place the authority wishes to see in the future (**Inset 18**). Using policy in this way will also ensure that the vision is subject to the widest possible debate, and subsequently forms the basis to guide both development activity and public sector investment. It is clear that authorities need to move beyond the notion that planning policy merely represents a means to control development, with policies based on ad hoc responses to particular problems, rather than as contributions to achieving a greater whole.

As a point of departure there is a need to clearly establish the design objectives for the area to be planned, for use in setting priorities for short-, medium- and long-term policy development. These might include something as fundamental as trying to inject a design dimension into regeneration objectives, or considering the role of design in an urban intensification or heritage conservation led strategy, through to the role of design within an overall commitment to sustainable development. What is important is that once established, the vision and policy objectives provide the appropriate hooks on which to hang more detailed policy in the range of action plans, including any authority-wide design statement (**Inset 19**). At this level, design policy should as a minimum articulate:

- the importance and weight attached to a proper understanding of context; and
- the conceptualisation of design adopted, indicating which are the key areas of design concern.

Inset 18: Defining a vision

The London Borough of **Camden's** community strategy — *Our Camden Our Future* — establishes a vision to address the huge inequalities in the Borough, in part by harnessing the equally huge opportunities. Six key aims are identified as well as 96 targets to ensure their delivery. The aims are:

- a place with stronger communities;
- a safer place;
- a healthier place;
- an economically successful place;
- an attractive and environmentally friendly place; and
- a place with excellent services.

Against each aim are listed the key plans and strategies for their implementation, with the UDP identified as the key delivery mechanism for an attractive and environmentally friendly place. For Camden, this component of their strategy involves better design, a greener environment, better traffic management, and the management of parks and public spaces. The vision for quality extends from delivering major developments, such as the regeneration of the Swiss Cottage area, to the complete refurbishment of many of Camden's world-renowned squares, the better control of parking, a biodiversity plan, and accessibility improvements for those with disabilities.

Inset 19: Providing hooks for design policy and guidance

Bristol is one of the few authorities to employ a single overarching policy for urban design. Policy B1 schedules seven design considerations with the first six elaborated separately in subsequent individual policies. The final consideration, environmental impact, is dealt with in the plan's 'Management of the Environment' chapter. The other considerations cover context, accessibility, safety, form, detail and sustainability. B1 was written to cover all forms of development and all geographical areas. The Bristol intention is to avoid a two-tier approach to policy, and to assert that the council's design expectations relate to the whole city district.

Policy B2 requires an appropriate response to local context, which is distinguished by scale. The justification splits developments into four categories — estate/large sites, streets, infill, and extensions — with the important characteristics of local context established for each. For example, issues identified at each scale include density, plot size, building rhythm, and architectural mouldings, respectively. Each policy is followed by a process-orientated implementation statement, which highlights relevant council actions and supplementary design guidance.

While Bristol has sometimes been criticised for having too many design policies, their approach reflects a wider strategy being considered for slimming down policy frameworks. Such overarching design policies act as potential policy hooks on which to hang secondary design policy and, potentially, other forms of design guidance as well. This approach is already adopted at **Birmingham** and is being considered by **Purbeck**.

Bristol, Investing in the public realm

Bristol: B1 Development: Design Criteria and Guidance

4.4.1 One of the aims of the Bristol Local Plan is to ensure that good quality design is given a high priority. In order to achieve this successfully, the city council will pursue, through negotiation and publication of supplementary guidance, a high standard of design in all new buildings and alterations to existing buildings. Policy B1, together with subsequent policies, outlines the broad principles and issues that will be taken into account in determining applications. Policies contained within Chapter 2 'Management of the Environment' should also be considered with regard to the design of buildings.

4.4.2 The design principles are developed further as supplementary planning guidance in the form of 'Policy Advice Notes' and 'Site Briefs' which offer design guidance and seek to clarify the expectations of the city council. In setting out criteria and offering guidance, the city council does not intend to establish rigid design principles, or to stifle architectural or artistic expression. It does, however, propose to safeguard basic amenity standards, while at the same time promoting sensitive design which respects and contributes to its surroundings.

B1 In determining applications, account will be taken of the following design issues:-

(i) **The local context**
(ii) **Accessibility**
(iii) **Safety and security**
(iv) **Layout and form**
(v) **Building exteriors and elevations**
(vi) **Landscape treatment and environmental works**
(vii) **Environmental impact**

Implementation: By use of planning guidance in the process of Development Control. Additional guidance may be produced as necessary.

It should also establish:

- a clear linkage between design and the delivery of sustainable development; and
- a broad authority-wide spatial strategy related to the authority's key strategic objectives.

7. Ensure that development responds appropriately to its context — visual, social, functional and environmental — as a fundamental policy objective

Ensuring that development responds appropriately to its context should be a fundamental objective of design policy. The advice in PPG1 (para. 18), PPG3 (para. 56) and PPG7 (para. 2.11) particularly stress the importance of local distinctiveness as the basis of design policy in urban, suburban and rural areas (**Inset 20**).

Inset 20: **Maintaining landscape distinctiveness**

Until recently **Bath** had one of the most holistic approaches to landscape found in any authority. The approach in Bath has been influenced by two primary concerns — the entire city's designation as a UNESCO World Heritage Site, and a broader concern for environmental management coupled with sustainable living. The streamlining of Bath's landscape policy framework represents a response to Government advice on shorter and clearer plans, but also to the city's amalgamation with Northeast Somerset. Nevertheless, Bath retains a unique landscape setting and urban form that demands careful attention to both the conservation of the Georgian and Victorian landscapes and enhancement of the natural landscape setting.

In response, Bath's landscape policy is more generic in nature and affords special protection to the landscape of AONB (area of outstanding natural beauty) status areas, urban landscapes, and the hillsides that give Bath so much of its character. Policy NE.3 'Important Hillsides' highlights the townscape contribution of views to the surrounding landscape and establishes the urban importance of Bath's green and rural setting. The urban landscape policy is set out in the 'Design and Urban Design' section of the plan in Policy D4 and D5. Policy D4 establishes that any proposed landscape should enhance development, with D5 requiring a design statement on landscape issues. Landscape policy is underpinned by *Cherishing Outdoor Places: A Landscape Strategy for Bath* (1993) which establishes a rigorous policy and management framework for the city's landscape areas. The city's response to a reduced local plan will also be an increased number of supplementary planning guides. As yet, officers are unsure if their new approach will sustain the high quality urban landscape because the new draft local plan has been neither adopted nor tested.

Bath: NE.3 Important Hillsides

C2.18 Within Bath, there are large tracts of open hillsides which are important in giving Bath its green and rural setting. Many are protected by Green Belt designation but Stirtingale Farm, Twerton Farm, The Tumps, Twerton Round Hill, Beechen Cliff, Lyncombe and Mount Beacon are not. These prominent, green hillsides within the built-up area are vital to the City's landscape setting and character. Many of the hillsides are also important for wildlife.

C2.19 Similarly Radstock's location at the convergence of five valleys contributes to its unique character. It is surrounded and penetrated by prominent hillsides which make a fundamental contribution to the town's character.

C2.20 These areas are shown on the Proposals Map and protected under Policy NE.3.

POLICY NE.3

Development that would adversely affect the landscape qualities of the important hillsides shown on the proposals map, or their contribution to the character and landscape setting of Bath and Radstock will not be permitted.

Bath, landscape and built form

However, context is not just a set of visual characteristics, and the appropriate response is not just a matter of relating a proposed development to the adjacent townscape. More fundamentally there is a need to relate development to its social, functional and environmental context and particularly to matters of movement and land use.

This implies a concern with issues of how the development relates to the social character of the locality, particularly how it affects the public realm, its vitality and safety, but also the more functional aspects of land-use relationships and linkages, and the flows of people and especially vehicles that new development generates (**Inset 21**). The environmental context emphasises the need to consider how new development affects natural environmental processes, reducing all forms of pollution and protecting biodiversity (see below).

Finally, while emphasising context there is still a need to recognise that this is never the only consideration in design, particularly at the architectural level, and that creativity and innovation can be equally important responding to technology, materials, building functions and architectural conventions (see below). Policy might spell out the circumstances under which site appraisals will be required with an application, and what such analysis should contain.

Inset 21: Addressing the local context

The **Leeds** Urban Design Strategy is underpinned by a comprehensive urban design analysis. Development of the city between the nineteenth century and 2000 is illustrated by two figure-ground studies and attention is drawn to the city's characteristic urban grain; a varied and flexible grid-iron street pattern. The form section includes a legibility analysis of the entire city centre, which highlights city-wide and other landmarks, and a range of views — views of city-wide landmarks, key views from outside the city centre, panoramic views, important local views and views in need of enhancement.

The city already uses this analysis in the determination of planning applications for tall buildings. In time this will be integrated into the city's spatial development strategy. Case studies include detailed analysis of specific areas and illustrative proposals for an area, in both two and three dimensions. Examples of successful developments and urban design details are shown in photographs. The authority see the strategy as the first in a series, all of which will involve participation of relevant interest,

professional and community groups in the production process. This first study was produced in collaboration with Leeds Metropolitan University with postgraduate urban design students undertaking much of the analysis. The strategy cross-references all the design policies in the development plan in an exemplary way, but the question remains as to how Leeds will slim down its very extensive range of policies.

Leeds, 'a space for relaxation and activity'

Leeds, 'Lynch Analysis'

8. Policies should be based on a broad concept of urban design that integrates built and natural environment concerns — sustainability is a fundamental design objective

The broader notion of context expressed above should also be reflected in the conceptualisation of design adopted in policy (see Chapter 5). Increasingly, national publications concerned with design advocate a compatible range of design principles (**Inset 22**). The significance is not in the exact wording of any of these (authorities should define what is important to them locally and thereby define their own agenda — **Inset 23**), but in the commonalities between them. They indicate that:

- design is being increasingly broadly defined;
- the significance of urban design (as opposed to architectural design) is increasingly emphasised;
- social and environmental dimensions are being considered alongside visual and functional concerns;
- the synergies between good design and the pursuit of sustainable development at large are accepted.

Inset 22: National design conceptualisations

	Towards an Urban Renaissance (1999)	*By Design, Urban Design in the Planning System* (2000)	*Urban Design Compendium* (2000)	*Better Places to Live, By Design* (2001)
Sustainable urban design	■ Building to last ■ Sustainable buildings ■ Environmental responsibility	■ Adaptability	■ Manage the investment ■ Design for change	■ Adaptability ■ Maintenance ■ Sustainability
Townscape	■ Context, scale and character	■ Character	■ Work with the landscape	■ Structure ■ Detail
Urban form	■ Optimising land use and density	■ Continuity and enclosure	■ Mix forms	■ Space
Public realm	■ Public realm	■ Quality of the public realm ■ Legibility	■ Places for people	■ Parking ■ Safety
Mixed use and tenure	■ Mixing activities ■ Mixing tenures	■ Diversity	■ Mix uses	■ Mix ■ Amenity ■ Community
Connection and movement	■ Access and permeability	■ Ease of movement	■ Make connections	■ Movement ■ Layout
Application to context	■ Site and setting	■ (Application through eight aspects of urban form)	■ Enrich the existing	■ Place

The emphasis on the environmental aspects of context implies the need to integrate built and natural environment concerns as a fundamental goal of design. Urban design remains dominated by a concern with existing built-up areas, their conservation and redevelopment, and the design principles that can be applied in such circumstances. While aspects of landscape have permeated design thought, they have tended to be superficial and largely cosmetic concerns, and little thought has been given to broader environmental considerations. Aspects of residential design have been particularly neglected, as has the whole question of how natural environmental assets and processes can be best protected in the conversion of land from rural to urban uses.

Inset 23: Developing an urban design agenda

The primary objective of the **Leeds** *City Centre Urban Design Strategy* is to help improve the quality of the built environment and specifically to create more 'people friendly' places. Officers intend to use their strategy to 'get ahead of developers' for the first time and to inform applicants of the standard of development required by the council. In this regard the authority believes that they are often on the back foot when a developer submits a proposal and hope the strategy will provide future applicants with a benchmark for development within the city. As supplementary design guidance, the strategy builds on design policies within the UDP, effectively acting as a guide to policy while setting specific objectives for development within the city. Policy N13 in the UDP, for example, states that good contemporary design which is sympathetic or complementary to its setting will be welcomed, while the strategy highlights the city's intention to promote high quality modern design.

Leeds' planners view the clarity of the wide-ranging urban design issues addressed in the strategy as fundamental to its success. Urban design issues are split into four themes (developed in-house), which will also form the basis for future design strategies:

- form (buildings and morphology);
- movement (vehicles and pedestrians);
- space (types and landscape); and
- use (activity and regeneration).

Each theme is subsequently defined by a series of keywords, the intention being to establish key components of each theme and highlight them to potential applicants. An extensive glossary of terms is also provided in the back of the document.

Officers acknowledge that there are complex inter-relationships between the themes and a balance will need to be struck in individual development proposals. Each theme broadly reflects the different contributions of key members of the development team — form relates mainly to architects, movement to highway engineers, space to landscape architects, and use to town planners. Although perhaps over-simplistic, the approach acknowledges the professional inter-relationships required for urban renaissance. Case studies then present typical developments that illustrate the council's aims. Leeds hope that applicants and their agents will learn from the key principles and case studies provided, and take them on board in future developments. Officers believe the *City Centre Urban Design Strategy* will reduce confrontation at the development control level and speed up the application process.

Leeds, positive corner/urban infill

Leeds, pulling together for city design

Inset 24: Sustainable development underpinning policy

Leicester cites sustainability as its core concern, with the plan paraphrasing the Bruntland definition and making reference to the Rio Earth Summit and the Kyoto agreement in its introduction. The aim of the plan is to facilitate the future development of Leicester in a sustainable manner. The city's sustainable agenda is second to none, reflecting their record as Britain's first 'Environment City'. Strategic theme ST01 states that the plan will promote the regeneration of the city, economically, socially, culturally and environmentally, to create a prosperous, civilised and attractive place for all its people. ST03: Quality Places is the overarching, criteria-based, urban design policy, which establishes sustainability as a primary development consideration.

The draft version of the plan was subject to a sustainability appraisal with the urban design section scoring highly across a range of indicators. Sustainable policies remain within the remit of planning and avoid the common overemphasis on detailed construction matters. Policy UD09 'Adaptability' impacts on the internal layout of buildings, although Leicester acknowledge that refusal of planning permission would be unlikely on these grounds alone. Nevertheless, they observe that the concern is identified in *By Design* and expect development control to use the policy in conjunction with other policy objectives. The council view UD09 as primarily an encouragement policy and aim to produce supplementary guidance on the issue in the future.

Birmingham's agenda is driven by their members' desire to create a more sustainable environment. While the city's 1993 plan never used the term 'sustainability', city planners argue that this was merely a question of terminology. In part, it reflected Birmingham's concern about sustainability being promoted as an almost exclusively environmental concern at the time, a view the city did not share. Today's broader ranging view of sustainability as focusing on the needs of people, both environmental and social, is considered more appropriate and is now built into the 2001 draft deposit UDP.

Leicester, sustainable architecture

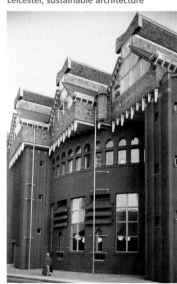

Chapter 3 'The Built Environment' establishes the 'Design Principles for Sustainable Development'. Issues addressed include layout, design, construction and consumption, while Policy 3.14E acts as a guiding principle for all development. Birmingham's six strong in-house urban design team generally assesses the environmental content of schemes, although external consultants are used if proposals are particularly large or complex. Birmingham stresses that sustainability and good design are viewed as two sides of the same coin, and neither takes precedence. Its strategy is to work with designers and developers to maximise both design quality and environmental sensitivity.

Leicester: ST01 The Overall Strategy

The City of Leicester Local Plan will promote the regeneration of the City, economically, socially, culturally and environmentally; creating a prosperous, civilised and attractive place for all its people. This will be achieved by managing change with integrity in accordance with the principles of quality and sustainability.

Equity

2.6 Many people take for granted their access to housing, employment and transport, as well as to a wide range of social, community and leisure facilities. It is crucial to their well being and quality of life. However the needs of disadvantaged people are often greater and their access to these staples less. It is vital that this is acknowledged in the Plan if progress towards social equity is to be made and social exclusion reduced. Of course the needs of different groups vary considerably and specific policies, for example on disabled persons' access, will be found in the body of the Plan.

Leicester: ST03 Quality Places

Development will be expected to demonstrate good urban design qualities. Planning permission for all major new development will only be given where it can be shown to:

- **improve the visual qualities of buildings in the city, the spaces they create, and the overall quality of people's surroundings;**
- **improve the vitality of the public realm, enable social and economic interaction and reduce the need to travel;**
- **improve the legibility of the city, create a sense of place, engender a strong positive identity and promote accessibility;**
- **minimise the consumption of energy and the production of waste and pollution;**
- **achieve imaginative and innovative mixed use development schemes, maximise the development potential of sites, and maintain environmental safeguards;**
- **address issues of biodiversity;**
- **incorporate works of art; and**
- **meet the needs of diverse communities, to secure equality of access and opportunity.**

2.8 Chapter 3 sets out the key urban design policies to be applied to all new development. These policies are amplified elsewhere in Supplementary Planning Guidance (SPG). See Appendix 01.

2.9 Achieving a higher quality urban environment will involve the City Council in providing guidance, setting standards and promoting innovation. However like many other ambitions of this Plan, it will only be achieved in partnership with others, notably those included in the development industry and local communities. PPG1 requires Local Planning Authorities to place the quality of design at the centre of its decision-making and the City Council will expect developers to produce 'Design Statements' to accompany all major planning applications. These should incorporate the principles described in policies ST03, ST04, ST05, ST06, ST07 and those of Chapter 3

Birmingham: 3.14E Design Principles for Sustainable Development

3.14E Development has a large impact on issues such as global warming, resource depletion and pollution. Developments, including new and refurbished buildings, should therefore be designed in a way which reduces such harmful impacts and respects the principles of a sustainable environment. Applications for development will be assessed against the following principles:

- Layouts should be designed to minimise reliance on the private car and encourage walking, cycling and the use of public transport;
- Existing buildings should be re-used wherever possible and where re-use would contribute to environmental quality;
- Consideration should be given to the use of environmentally friendly materials, including the re-use of materials, where appropriate;
- The orientation, external and internal design of buildings, and use of landscaping, should maximise the use of natural heat and light, contribute to local biodiversity and minimise the use of non-renewable energy sources. The use of renewable energy sources will be actively encouraged. This should not, however, be at the expense of good urban design;
- Good thermal and noise insulation should be provided;
- Consideration should be given to the use of higher densities and more compact layouts where they will not conflict with other Plan policies or with other good urban design principles;
  Consideration should be given to measures that will minimise the consumption of water, for example by the re-use of grey water and water saving devices and practices. Further policies on sustainable use of water and sustainable drainage are included in paragraphs 3.71–3.76;
- Buildings should be long-life and flexible and capable of being adapted for a variety of other uses with the minimum of disruption;
- Any contamination on a site should be assessed, and if necessary, remediation work carried out to ensure that the site is fit for the use for which it is intended.

Inset 25: Sustainable design by spatial scale (Carmona, M. in Layard _et al._, 2001)

	Buildings	Spaces	Quarters	Settlements
Stewardship	Responding to and enhancing context Design for easy maintenance	Responding to and enhancing context Managing the public realm Allowing personalisation of public space Traffic calming	Design for revitalisation Developing a long-term vision Investing necessary resources	'Joining-up' contributions to quality — design, planning, transport, urban management Governance that supports stakeholder involvement
Resource efficiency	Using passive (and active) solar gain technologies Design for energy retention Reduce embodied energy — local materials and low energy materials Use recycled and renewable materials Design for natural light and ventilation	Layouts to allow sun penetration Spaces that reduce vehicle speeds and restrict vehicle circulation Design spaces that reduce wind speeds and enhance microclimate Using local, natural materials	Reduced parking standards Urban block depths that allow sun and natural light penetration and which encourage natural ventilation Using combined heat and power systems Local access to public transport	Investing in public transport infrastructure Utilise more efficiently before extending the established capital web (infrastructure)
Diversity and choice	Provide opportunity to mix uses within buildings Mix building types, ages and tenures Build accessible, lifetime homes and buildings	Mix uses along streets and in blocks Design for walking and cycling Combat privatisation of the public realm Remove barriers to local accessibility	Mix uses within quarters Design a fine-grained street and space network (micro scale) Support diversity in neighbourhood character Localise facilities and services	Integrate travel modes Connect route networks (macro scale) Centre hierarchy to boost choice Variety in services and facilities between centres Remove barriers to accessibility
Human needs	Support innovation and artistic expression in design Design to a human scale Design visually interesting buildings	Provide high quality, imageable, public spaces Combat crime through space design and management Enhance safely by reducing pedestrian/vehicle conflict Design for social contact and for safe children's play	Design visually interesting networks of space Enhance legibility through landmark and space disposition Socially mix communities	Enhance legibility through quarter identity and disposition Promote equity through land use disposition Build settlement image to foster sense of belonging
Resilience	Build extendible buildings Build adaptable buildings Build to last Use resilient materials	Design robust spaces, usable for many functions Design spaces able to accommodate above and below ground infrastructure requirements Design of serviceable space	Design to allow fine-grained changes of use across districts Robust urban block layouts	Build a robust capital web — infrastructure to last and adapt Recognise changing patterns of living and work
Pollution reduction	Reuse and recycle waste water Insulate for reduced noise transmission — vertically and horizontally On-site foul water treatment	Reduce hard surfaces and runoff Design in recycling facilities Design well ventilated space to prevent pollution build-up Give public transport priority	Match projected CO_2 emissions with tree planting Plant trees to reduce pollution Tackle light pollution	Question 'end-of-pipe' solutions to water/sewerage disposal Control private motorised transport Clean and constantly maintain the city
Concentration	Design compact building forms to reduce heat loss, i.e. terraces Bring derelict buildings back into use Consider high buildings where appropriate	Reduce space given over to roads Reduce space given over to parking Increase vitality through activity concentration	Intensify around transport intersections Raise density standards and avoid low-density building Build at densities able to support a viable range of uses and facilities Respect privacy and security needs	Enforce urban containment and reduce expansion Intensify along transport corridors Link centres of high activity
Distinctiveness	Reflect surrounding architectural character in design Enhance locally distinctive building settings Retain important buildings	Reflect urban form, townscape and site character in design Retain distinctive site features Design for sense of place — local distinctiveness Retain important building groups and spaces	Reflect morphological patterns and history — incremental or planned Identify and reflect significant public associations Consider quarter uses and qualities	Protect any positive regional identity and landscape character Utilise topographical setting Preserve archaeological inheritance
Biotic support	Provide opportunities for greening buildings Consider buildings as habitats	Design in robust soft landscaping Plant and renew street trees Encourage greening and display of private gardens	Provide minimum public open space standards Provide private open space Create new or enhancing existing habitats Respect natural features	Link public (and private) open space into a network Green urban fringe locations Integrate town and country Support indigenous species
Self sufficiency	Demonstrate a sense of public sector civic responsibility Encourage private sector civic responsibility Provide bicycle storage Connecting to the internet	Encourage self-policing through design Providing space for small-scale trading Provide bicycle parking facilities	Build a sense of community Involve communities in decision-making Encourage local food production — allotments, gardens, urban farms Paying locally for any harm	Encourage environmental literacy through example and promotion Consultation and participation in vision making and design

The concept of sustainability implies a much more profound basis for the relationship between the built and natural worlds, and the need to consider carefully the natural processes of the locality (hydrology, ecology, wildlife, micro-climate and air quality/filtration) and its consumption of resources (particularly energy and raw materials) at both the local and global scales. It requires a particular focus upon issues of biodiversity (the resources of the natural world) and upon the efficient use of energy, both in terms of travel and domestic/industrial consumption. The goal of sustainability needs to inform almost every design policy from considerations of density and mixed-use through to the use of particular materials in building, or the choice of species in landscape design. It also implies a concern for social and economic sustainability where good quality urban design has an important role to play in promoting social inclusion and lasting economic regeneration (**Inset 24**).

Inset 25 indicates the wide range of concerns covered by a more fundamental view of sustainability and the impact of sustainable thinking on design across a range of spatial scales. It helps to demonstrate that:

- a concern with sustainable design extends well beyond building design;
- tensions may sometimes exist between different sustainable design objectives — for example between orientation to maximise solar gain and contextual fit — and that a common sense approach to resolving such issues is required based on the nature of the context;
- the achievement of sustainable development and good urban design are intimately bound together and should not be seen as separate objectives.

9. Authorities should develop a clear spatial design strategy at authority-wide and area-wide scales that should be related to their key strategic objectives

For too long design has been regarded as purely a site-specific, micro-scale concern, and its role in shaping overall urban form and the pattern of urban development has been ignored. In most of Europe large-scale but detailed land-use plans set out the future patterns of land use and define the 'capital web' — the nature and location of major infrastructure investments. Significantly, these plans are legally binding on the public authorities who provide the infrastructure. They provide both a framework for private investment decisions and a mechanism for the conservation of key natural and built resources.

In the UK, the strategic concept of urban design should be articulated at a local authority-wide scale embracing individual districts or neighbourhoods. The required proposals map in the proposals section of the LDF, and the key diagram in the core strategy, offer the ideal opportunities to articulate a clear strategy in terms of growth (development), infrastructure investment, open space provision and conservation (**Inset 26**). Such strategies might then be linked to more detailed, area-specific spatial design strategies through action plans and other non-statutory documents as a means to spell out the district-wide spatial strategy at the intermediate and local scales.

Inset 26: Developing a strategic framework

The London Borough of **Lambeth** has called its recently adopted UDP 'the first green paper-friendly development plan in the country' (*Planning*, 4 January 2002). The plan is one of the shortest in London and contains both a spatial development strategy and core policies. The key diagram is a visual representation of the main elements of the plan's strategy, including how it relates to adjoining boroughs. Lambeth's diagram also highlights key strategic designations and proposals, including metropolitan open land, district centres, major town centres, transport development areas and major public transport proposals. Thus, although solely transport based, the proposals begin to relate key infrastructure investments to significant statutory designations.

Core policies are developed in Lambeth's vision for the borough, which sets spatial priorities for development and regeneration. The aim of the core strategic policies is to provide a comprehensive yet concise set of policies to be used as a basis for assessing the impact of specific planning applications on key plan objectives. In total, the 'Core Strategic Policies' section contains just three policies. Policy 1 'The vision for Lambeth' promotes sustainable development and urban renaissance within a social context. The policy focuses on the impact of development at both the local and global level, and emphasises the importance of good public transport links for area regeneration. Policy 2 focuses on the 'London South-Central' regeneration project and intends to promote development of an integrated 'heart' of London with the Thames as a unifying feature. Again, policy focuses heavily on transport and cross-river transport links. The justification for Policy 2 confirms that most of the South Bank plays little or no part in London as a world city and contains some of the most deprived communities in the capital. Policy 3 addresses the 'Central London Policy Area' and establishes that planning permission will be refused if development results in the loss of core central London activities or supporting activities where these contribute to the character and function of the area.

Lambeth: Policy 1 The Vision for Lambeth

To promote sustainable development and urban renaissance by making Lambeth a great place to live, visit and work.

The spatial priorities for development and regeneration will be:

- Maximising the opportunities for residents and others from Lambeth's location at the heart of a world city, through improved employment opportunities and better public transport links; and
- Ensuring safe, inclusive, mixed, livable and balanced communities — in particular giving priority to protecting residential amenity, providing more affordable housing and the regeneration of Lambeth's most deprived communities.

Applications should be accompanied by adequate supporting information showing how the proposal comprehensively addresses any potential adverse environmental or other impact, having regard to the policies of the plan.

4.3.1. This is the overarching policy that crystallizes the overall strategy of the plan. The Council's vision statement and the community plan set the overall goals for Lambeth. This plan, and in particular this policy, provide the spatial expression of this — how priorities and locations for land-use will help achieve this vision. At its heart is the central importance of achieving sustainable development.

4.3.2. The Urban White Paper 'Our Towns and Cities: The Future Delivering an Urban Renaissance Nov 2000' outlines the government's overall policies towards urban areas. The concept of urban renaissance concerns the rediscovery of the opportunities offered by cities to sensibly accommodate changing population, work and leisure patterns through the creation of practical, attractive, safe and efficient urban areas which offer a vibrant and desirable quality of life.

Lambeth, strategic development strategy

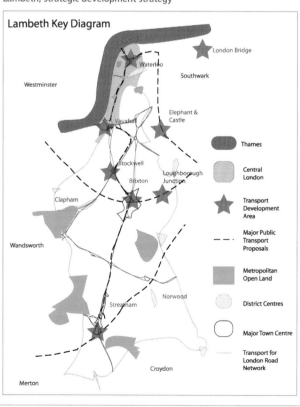

But strategic design is not merely a matter of thinking of design at different spatial scales. Design objectives need to be related to the key vision or objectives of policy, whether it is regeneration, conservation, urban containment, or urban/regional growth management. Teasing out the design dimension of such policies, and clearly identifying what environmental benefits are being sought and why, will make them much more effective and more widely supported; not least because the environmental implications and benefits can be articulated more clearly. Identifying the key design considerations that will underpin design at each scale, and how they interlock one with another, will allow a much more integrated and effective approach to achieving design quality in the round.

Watch points

- **Beware of undermining policy coverage.** Ensure that overarching design policies still address all key design concerns and provide the hooks from which to develop more detailed policy elsewhere.
- **Involve the community in vision making.** Involvement of others (the community and development interests) from the start in establishing the design vision may save much time later in explaining and defending it.
- **Involve the community in appraisal.** Once a robust methodology has been developed, appraisals can also involve a wide range of interests, the community, development interests, local universities, students on summer jobs, junior staff and so forth. They are not necessarily prohibitively expensive and time consuming.
- **Different contexts require different policy responses.** Design policy should relate to the whole urban environment. Avoid creating arbitrary boundaries and think in context.
- **Integrate sustainability.** Sustainability objectives too often lack substance and precision. Ensure policy highlights a strategic approach to the issue and fully integrate sustainability and design policy objectives.
- **Avoid getting bogged down with the detail.** It is important to deal with the fundamentals before the details. Planning has often been criticised for an over-concern with the latter to the exclusion of the former.
- **Spatial development strategies should move beyond analysis.** Strategies are about establishing a positive vision for change, not about describing the status quo.
- **Spatial strategies should consider more than transport.** Ensure that key strategic diagrams highlight key development, regeneration, infrastructure, open space and conservation proposals and opportunities, as well as important views and vistas or other designations. The integration of transport, density and land use matters is critical.
- **Strategies should make connections**. No place exists as an independent entity and strategies need to relate to their wider context and neighbouring areas.

5

Key aspects of design policy coverage

Key aspects of design policy coverage

Scales of intervention

The above recommendations constitute some of the fundamentals of design policy writing and apply across the range of design policies. In particular, they should be reflected in the LDF core strategy. It is now possible to move on to a more comprehensive design agenda and to highlight key recommendations (**Figure 4**).

These recommendations relate to the city/authority-wide scale (see Chapter 4), move through the intermediate scale of landscape and urban design considerations to the detailed issues of architecture and urban management. All are important in the pursuit of better quality development and although the emphasis and degrees of detail will change, authorities should ensure they adequately address design across strategic, intermediate and detailed scales of intervention and across their geographic area. To begin, it is strongly recommended that authorities prepare an authority-wide design statement (see Chapter 3) in which the following issues should be fully addressed. They should build on the range of fundamental design concerns already discussed, and in doing so build logically on policy established in their core strategy.

10. Urban design policies embracing townscape, urban form, public realm, mixed use and layout and movement considerations should be the cornerstone of design policies

It bears restatement that design control needs to go beyond a concern with the external appearance of development, to embrace the social, functional and environmental aspects of design, and a concern with the quality of public spaces and streets created by new development (**Inset 27**). The failure to positively shape the public realm has been the consequence of a focus on individual acts of building, highway engineering and environmental management rather than their collective impact upon streets and public spaces as a whole. It has also been the unfortunate outcome of the various incomplete syntheses of design adopted in the past by all the key professional and governmental participants in the planning and development process.

The dominance of the townscape philosophy, with its focus on the visual relationships between buildings, the maintenance of historic and architectural character, and the protection of views and vistas, has been partly responsible for the preoccupation with external appearance and

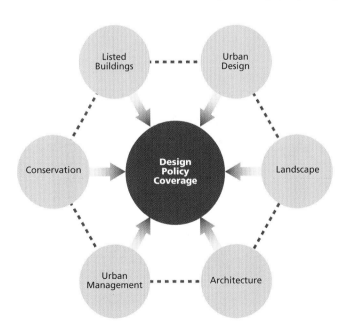

Figure 4: Design policy coverage

architecture in British planning practice at the expense of public space. Such concerns remain important and should be reflected in policy (**Inset 28**). Nevertheless, the townscape approach should be complemented by a concern with

Inset 27: A broad urban design agenda

Birmingham has a reputation of being one of the most innovative British cities as regards urban design. Policy 3.14D highlights a series of 'Good Urban Design Principles' against which applications for new development can be assessed. The policy avoids issues of architectural detail and instead focuses on issues of urban design — context, scale, design, permeability, mixed use, safety and landscape — for which criteria-based policies are developed. Conceptually, the policy is intended to provide a methodology for design rather than creating a prescriptive set of rules. As such, Policy 3.14D reflects Birmingham's holistic approach to new development. It complements Policy 3.14E 'Design Principles for Sustainable Development' (see **Inset 24**) which links design to sustainability at a variety of levels, for example, that layouts should be designed to minimise reliance on the private car, and orientation should maximise the use of natural heat and light.

The structure of the policy deliberately brings a series of urban design concepts together and sets them in tension, i.e. the need for permeability versus layouts that maximise solar gain. This approach establishes that design compromises may be required. Nevertheless, the overarching design policy provides a framework for managing this change. Design policies are expanded in a sophisticated range of supplementary design guidance and area frameworks, and are complemented in the plan by constituency statements, which add design detail for specific areas.

Birmingham: 3.14D Good Urban Design Principles

3.14D Applications for new development will be assessed against the following principles:

■ The City Council will have particular regard towards the impact that the proposed development would have on the local character of an area, including topography, street patterns, building lines, boundary treatments, views, skyline, open spaces and landscape, scale and massing, and neighbouring uses;

■ Local characteristics which are considered detrimental in terms of urban design and which undermine the overall character of the area should not be used as a precedent for the design of new developments; for example, buildings that back onto the public realm;

■ The scale and design of new buildings and spaces should generally respect the area surrounding them, and should reinforce and evolve any characteristics, including natural features such as watercourses, which are considered to be positive;

■ People should be able to move around freely, easily and safely throughout the City: therefore in new developments, streets and routes should generally link up rather than take the form of culs-de-sac and dead ends;

■ Mixed uses will be encouraged in centres, and in other areas where they can contribute towards meeting an identified local need;

■ To ensure that places feel safe, pleasant and legible, the fronts and backs of buildings should be clearly defined. Windows and more active rooms should face the public realm and main entrances should open onto the public realm, whereas the backs of buildings should be private and face other backs;

■ Landscaping should be an integral part of all major development proposals, and this should be designed to complement the new development and the surrounding area;

■ Any existing mature trees should be retained where possible, and the planting of new trees will be required where appropriate in accordance with the policy set out in paragraph 3.16A below.

Birmingham, Bullring redevelopment

Birmingham, new connections at Brindleyplace

Inset 28: Townscape differentiation policies

The city of **Westminster's** plan has one of the most sophisticated contextually based approaches to townscape. Policy DES 4 highlights a range of discrete architectural and urban design parameters for infill development in three types of area: varied townscape of significant quality; unified townscape of significant quality; and varied townscape of low quality. The most stringent control of development is applied in areas of unified townscape of significant quality, and here scholarly replicas of the predominant pattern are required. Most design freedom is permitted in areas of varied townscape of low quality, and here independence of form is a critical issue. Contemporary design is also promoted in such locations. Areas of varied townscape of significant quality are controlled by a contextual approach, with policy highlighting the importance of responding to the existing scale, massing, plot widths and architectural characteristics of adjoining buildings. In such locations the predominant residential density of an area should also guide development.

The application of DES 4 is intended to reflect Westminster's view that the higher the quality and more unified the character of the townscape, the greater the respect for the original scale, form and materials that is required. Officers observe that it is

Westminster's intention through their urban design policies to develop a series of policies that work through the scales, from the macro to the micro, and to one-off special projects. Policy success is reflected in numerous Civic Trust and other design awards for schemes within the borough.

The London Borough of **Haringey** follows Westminster's approach by modelling their policy DES 1.2 'Assessment of Design (1): Fitting New Buildings into the Surrounding Area' on Westminster's DES 4. Haringey's policy sets the design parameters for infill development in three types of area, with the variety and quality of townscape being the determining factors. Westminster originally adopted this approach but now structures the three types of area in accordance with their relative prevalence in the city.

Westminster, National Portrait Gallery design assessment

Westminster: DES 4 Infill Development

Aim
10.30 To ensure the highest quality of new development in order to preserve or enhance Westminster's townscape.

POLICY DES 4: INFILL DEVELOPMENT

(A) Varied townscape of significant quality
Permission will be granted in areas of varied townscape of significant quality, including conservation areas and Thames-side areas, where the form and design of the new infill development are disciplined by the:

1. building lines and scale of the area;
2. heights and massing of adjoining buildings;
3. characteristic building plot widths of the area;
4. architectural characteristics, profile and silhouette of adjoining buildings;
5. type, colour and origin of materials of adjoining buildings;
6. complexity and richness of materials, form and detailing of existing buildings which contribute positively to the character and appearance of the area;
7. the predominant residential density of the area (in the case of residential schemes).

(B) Unified townscape of significant quality
Permission will not normally be granted in terraces or groups of buildings of unified townscape of significant quality for new infill developments unless they are designed as scholarly replicas of the predominant pattern.

(C) Varied townscapes of low quality
Permission will be granted in areas of low quality varied townscape for new infill developments that:

1. have sufficient independence of form and contemporary design to create new compositions and points of interest;
2. respect existing building lines;
3. conform to the overall scale of the area;
4. have regard to the form and materials of adjoining building;
5. respect the predominant residential density of the area (in the case of residential schemes).

Policy application
10.31 Infill development is well suited to the small scale and varied townscape character of the City of Westminster. Its form should be determined by its townscape context. The higher the quality and more unified the character of the townscape, the greater the respect for the original scale, form and materials that should be shown by new developments.

10.32 Within areas of high-quality varied townscape, developments should be integrated into their surroundings. This will be achieved through the appropriate choices of scale, form and materials that reflect the type and quality of the existing townscape. Good modern design may be acceptable for infill developments, if successfully carried out within the criteria set out in the policy.

10.32a In areas of unified townscape of significant quality, scholarly replica rebuilding will be sought. For example, in order to restore or complete an otherwise coherent, distinctive piece of townscape, or where a building of historic or townscape value has been lost.

10.33 In areas of low-quality varied townscape, new developments should positively improve the quality of the area. The opportunity exists to generate new compositions and points of interest. High quality innovative modern architecture may be acceptable in such locations, provided that it respects the scale and form of their surroundings.

10.33a The City Council's relevant supplementary planning guidance with respect to the design of new building in the city is 'Design Matters in Westminster' (2001).

10.33b The City Council's relevant supplementary planning guidance with respect to infill development in conservation areas is set out in 'Development and Demolition in Conservation Areas' (1996).

Reason
10.34 The form of new development will affect the townscape quality of the City in the future. It should therefore be permitted only in areas where it will be beneficial, and its relationship with its surroundings should be carefully controlled.

Inset 29: Public realm policies

The London Borough of **Wandsworth's** approach to design is predicated on the belief that public realm issues are of greater concern to a planning department and are more important in achieving a successful built environment than visual architectural or townscape concerns. The latter are also much harder for an authority to control. Public realm policies TBE5–TBE10 deal with accessibility, physical integration, safety, desire lines, building lines, public/private interfaces, visual linking between buildings and public space, and ground floor activity. The policies attempt to address front–back incompatibilities, secure a more animated public realm and consider the relationships between buildings and the street. The intention is to ensure that doors and windows overlook public spaces, that access to the ground and upper floors are directly to the street, and that development delivers perimeter block forms of development with secure permeable routes, rather than cul-de-sacs. Wandsworth intend to avoid the development of buildings that are isolated from the street scene.

Wandsworth, considering the public/private interface

Policies TBE5–TBE10 have been in place since 1992 with only minor amendments. For example, revised TBE 7 increases the emphasis on public space in large development and sustainability. The policy

Wandsworth, articulating the public realm

highlights that layout and orientation should maximise opportunities for energy conservation and that large development should include public spaces. Other public realm policies have been subject to minor wording changes, which are intended to make them more deliverable and easier to defend at appeal. Each policy element has been fully tested and considered effective in delivering their objectives.

Wandsworth: Layout and Form of Development: TBE 5–TB10

Policy TBE5   New developments should be physically integrated into their surroundings by preserving and extending links with existing public routes. Safe and attractive through public routes, appropriate to the size of the development and the grain of the surrounding area, and related to existing desire lines and any new ones arising from the development, should be included to maintain a high level of permeability. Developments should be laid out so as to facilitate safe and convenient access and movement by pedestrians and cyclists, both within the development and between the development and the surrounding areas.

Policy TBE6   New developments in existing streets should maintain the prevailing building line with building frontages (see policy TBE9). Discontinuities in the building line should demonstrate benefits to the quality of the public space. Where there are no established building lines, streets and other public spaces should be similarly defined by new building frontages.

Policy TBE7   Developments should be designed so that buildings contribute collectively through their siting and massing to the spaces they define. Large developments should include public spaces, which should be designed to allow sunlight to penetrate and to avoid generating excessive windspeeds. The layout and orientation of buildings should where possible take account of opportunities to maximise energy conservation.

Policy TBE8   There should be a clear relationship between public space and private space where the maintenance of privacy and security does not prejudice the quality of the public space. Private spaces (e.g. rear gardens) adjoining streets and other public spaces should be avoided where possible. Semi-private space (e.g. forecourts) providing a transition between buildings and public spaces should be defined by low walls, fences or railings.

Policy TBE9   Frontages to streets and other public spaces should incorporate doors and windows to provide physical and visual links between the building and the public space.

Policy TBE10 Activity-generating uses should be included on the ground floor of new developments, especially at focal points of pedestrian movement.

Inset 30: Reflecting community aspirations and social equity

Sheffield has a clear plan strategy based on equal opportunities and quality of life. The city's primary concern is therefore to ensure that proposals do not worsen the living conditions of disadvantaged people more than those of powerful, articulate or wealthy groups. Strategic Policy SP1 'A City for People' provides the overarching theme of the UDP, and establishes a range of city-wide considerations. SP1 is reinforced by Policy SP3 'A City Centre for People', which focuses on the role of the centre in the regeneration and life of the city as a whole. **Leicester** also sees equality as of primary importance. At the strategic level, the city establishes that all development proposals need to take account of the special needs of disadvantaged people in an attempt to advance social equity. Both cities translate issues of social equity into planning policy at the strategic level. Sheffield's policy focuses on ensuring that development creates safer and more attractive places, while Leicester take the more global stance of expecting development to improve the overall quality of people's surroundings.

Sheffield's approach is grounded in community aspirations. The first draft was developed in consultation with various advisory groups set up specifically to cater for disadvantaged areas and client groups. Most of the groups were drawn from particular geographical areas but five represented particular city-wide interests. For the first review, consultations have been primarily geographically based on twelve permanent area panels, and specific client groups will be reached through representative organisations rather than by setting up new groups. Sheffield's vision is to work with the community to regenerate the city and to improve the quality of life for all its residents.

The orientation of policy towards particular groups is achieved in the 'What the plan does for disadvantaged people' chapter. This chapter does not establish new policy but is intended to allow certain groups — people with disabilities, older people, ethnic minorities, women, people with children, unemployed people, homeless people, other people on low incomes, people in areas of poverty, and young people — to identify policies that are particularly relevant to them. For those with disabilities, for example, key design-related concerns highlighted include accessibility, safety and security and the design of public buildings, access standards to buildings, design for vehicles and parking, and the design of the streetscape. Sheffield understands that the UDP will be just one contribution to bridging the gap between the city's poor and better off, but it sets out the city's stall as far as values, aims and aspirations are concerned.

Sheffield: SP1 A City For People

A balance will be struck between competing land uses, and between new development, conservation and transport, which would:

(a) **best meet the needs of the people of the City for houses, jobs, leisure and services; and**
(b) **meet the needs of the present without compromising the ability of future generations to meet their own needs; and**
(c) **give priority, wherever possible, to run-down areas and to meeting the needs of disadvantaged people; and**
(d) **lead to a healthier, safer, more convenient and more attractive environment; and**
(e) **protect and enhance the natural and built heritage of the City; and**
(f) **promote the re-use of urban land for development wherever practicable while allowing greenfield developments on allocated sites; and**
(g) **lead to a high quality environment which would promote economic development; and**
(h) **integrate land use and transport to reduce the distances people need to travel wherever possible; and**
(i) **allow public transport to be operated efficiently; and**
(j) **contribute to the social, economic and environmental regeneration of the City.**

Reasons for the Policy
The Policy draws on the main themes of the strategy and the ways in which the different aims may complement each other (see pages 9–14, 29–34).

How it will be put into practice
By:

Deciding planning applications.

Providing advice to developers, which could include supplementary planning guidance or planning briefs.

Identifying and promoting sites suitable for development.

Consulting with local residents, community groups and developers.

Evaluating all proposed developments in terms of their impact on the environment and on disadvantaged people and taking account of such impact in making planning decisions.

Putting into practice the more detailed Policies and proposals of the Plan.

Sheffield, Peace Gardens

Sheffield, Peace Gardens at night

the accessibility, legibility, vitality, safety and comfort of the public realm, its role as a container of activities and setting for human behaviour, as well as its ability to promote walking and cycling (**Inset 29**). Issues of community aspirations, identity and cultural expression are also part of this concern (**Inset 30**).

Inset 31: A suggested agenda for urban design policies

Sustainable Urban Design
- A comprehensive definition of urban design should underpin the structure and content of design policies whether in urban or rural areas. It should embrace issues of townscape, urban form, public realm, mixed use and tenure, connection and movement, and the application of key design principles to different contexts.
- Sustainable development should be a principal goal of urban design at all scales — buildings, spaces, quarters and settlements (see **Inset 25**) — and should take into account both differential environmental capacities and sustainable patterns of development form.

Townscape (visual composition of space)
- Townscape policies should be used to embrace a concern with the visual relationships of a development to its site and its wider setting, and to define the appropriate townscape role of a development, including its relationship to, and provision of, visually interesting public space and buildings.
- The protection of both local and strategic views represents an important element of townscape policy, particularly where topographic or historic factors have combined to create particular assets of the skyline or the natural setting of a settlement.
- Local planning authorities can usefully support the provision of high quality hard landscape — paving, boundary treatments, street furniture, signage, lighting and public art (see **Inset 36**) — in all new development in order to enhance the streetscape.

Urban form (three-dimensional built volume)
- Urban form policies should seek an appropriate scale of development through control of the building envelope incorporating density, height, and massing concerns, but emphasising the creation of a human scale consistent with the context.
- Key character-giving elements will be the relative enclosure of public spaces and continuity of the building line, as well as the diversity and pattern of the established urban grain and block and plot sizes.
- Density allocations in existing urban areas should be carefully tailored to the existing character of the area and to relative accessibility, and should not override other key contextual considerations. The exception is where major redevelopment is envisaged, and here such allocations need to be related to dimensional criteria that will define the broad building envelope and its relationship to public space.
- Urban form policies should include considerations of sunlight, daylight, and microclimate to ensure good living and working conditions, comfortable public spaces and energy conservation.

Public realm (the social experience)
- Public realm policies can complement townscape and urban form policies by encouraging legible, comfortable, stimulating and safe streets and public spaces. A key aim should be the encouragement of active frontages at ground level wherever feasible.
- Policy should incorporate public perceptions of what is important in the identity and quality of the built environment, and incorporate these into design strategies and individual policies.

Inset 31 outlines a suggested agenda for urban design policy, while the various conceptualisations in Inset 22 identify others. The important point is to ensure a systematic coverage of the urban design agenda, and to relate that agenda to the locality.

- Public realm policies should embrace design-against-crime principles including considerations of defensible space, surveillance, visibility, lighting, and other security measures.
- Functional concerns, such as parking and servicing, should be considered with a view to minimising their impact on the public realm and meeting other urban design and sustainable objectives.

Mixed use and tenure
- The mixing of uses should be a fundamental policy objective, in order to create more sustainable living and movement patterns, and more vital and viable urban centres.
- Policies should encourage the creation of sustainable communities through support for mixing tenures and designs that permit a variety of tenure types.
- In residential developments, the provision of adequate and attractive private amenity spaces with a minimum of overlooking should be a key objective, as well as public open spaces suitably equipped for sport and play.

Connection and movement
- Accessibility considerations will be important to the detailed design of public space and to ensuring that all groups can easily use and move through space. Visual and physical permeability will be of primary importance.
- Policies should seek to promote walking and cycling as the most sustainable modes of transport, and ensure the quality of both through frontage controls and a network of enhancement schemes.
- Residential layouts should seek to maximise the level of local autonomy for residents, structure development around energy efficient movement networks, and use landscape and open space to serve ecological and anti-pollution purposes.
- Road layouts should prioritise safe, easy and direct pedestrian movement and the creation of a network of attractive, well connected public space, while being aware of the need for convenience for the private motorist. The 'Companion Guide' to Design Bulletin 32 'Residential Roads and Footpaths' (1998) offers valuable guidance in this regard.

Application to context
- Policy should aim to enhance the unique qualities of different places through addressing the range of policy areas outlined above and applying them to different contexts through area and site-specific guidance and development control.
- Particular contexts within an authority may merit the development of specific policies and design strategies. These include countryside, urban fringe, town centres, residential areas, waterways and other areas with a strong identity. These will provide opportunities for tailoring landscape/townscape, urban form, and public realm policies to the nature of the locality.
- Policies for particular types of development offer a useful way of responding to recurrent design problems and expressing accumulated design experience (see **Inset 10**).
- Policies for different scales of development provide a means of highlighting the different concerns of large-, medium- and small-scale developments and their relationship to site and surroundings.

11. Considerations of landscape should pervade policies at all scales of design and will be a critical element of sustainable development

Landscape policies have remained poorly developed in development plans and in their place a few token mentions of 'landscaping' are usually included. Even the latter are usually identified as reserved matters to be resolved once planning permission has been granted. It is argued that landscape policies are fundamental at both the strategic and local levels; in the former in defining those areas for conservation or development as open space for hydrological, ecological, aesthetic or amenity reasons, and in the latter in ensuring that key landscape features on

Inset 32: Protecting open space of townscape importance

The London Borough of **Richmond's** UDP has a strong environmental theme with comprehensive landscape and open space policies. Policies are located in the 'Open Environment' chapter, which precedes the built environment section and promotes the significance of landscape within the plan. Policies are kept brief with much of the detail placed in the justification. Policy ENV 3 'Other Open Land of Townscape Importance' highlights the role of open space in creating townscape character.

Richmond developed ENV 3 because not every piece of open space that contributes to the urban environment can be designated as metropolitan open land or classified as greenbelt. The authority also wished to avoid a two-tier system for the protection of open land, and sought to prevent hard and fast distinctions between conservation and non-conservation areas. Policy justification highlights the local significance of pockets of greenery and their value in creating local character. Thus, Richmond's plan attempts to spread the

protection of open land as broadly as possible and to create a holistic approach to the environment rather than just protecting the 'jewels in the crown'. Areas protected by policy ENV 3 are often owned by the London Borough of Richmond and in some cases this policy has been used to protect the council from itself — Richmond is under extreme pressure to develop such pockets of urban space for new schools.

Richmond: ENV 3 Other Land of Townscape Importance

5.34 **The Council will protect and *seek* to enhance other open areas that are of townscape importance. In considering development on sites adjoining these open areas the Council will take into account any possible visual impact on the character of the open land.**

5.35 In some parts of the Borough, open areas, which are not extensive enough to be defined as green belt or metropolitan open land, act as pockets of greenery of local rather than London-wide significance. Many of these are of townscape importance, contributing to the local character and are valued by residents as open spaces in the built up area. These areas include public and private sports grounds, some school playing fields, cemeteries, some large private gardens and some allotments, all of which the Secretary of State for the Environment has recognised can be of great importance to the character of a neighbourhood. *LPAC through work on urban green space also recognises the importance of such land.* The larger areas are shown on the proposals map but there will be other smaller areas which merit protection. The purpose of this policy is to safeguard open land and ensure that it is not lost to other uses without good cause. The policy recognises that there may be exceptional cases where it would be appropriate to allow modest buildings and extensions which are related to the function of Other Open Land of Townscape Importance (OOLTI) and when this would not have a harmful effect on its character.

Richmond Upon Thames, protecting 'ordinary' green space

particular sites are protected and the development is best sited to take advantage of and maintain landscape qualities and character.

Landscape as a resource is seen as a central pillar of sustainability policies and it is landscape as a natural resource rather than landscape as purely visual scenery, which should be the focus of policy. Through landscape policies, the best natural features of the area should be protected, biodiversity ensured and minimum damage ensue to the natural processes of the site (**Inset 32**). Landscape policies need to be considered (particularly in action plans) alongside the provision of open space and recreation facilities (**Inset 33**), and to be given a stronger ecological dimension as well as more workable means of implementation

Inset 33: Landscape in development

The London Borough of **Haringey** sees both hard and soft landscaping as a critical design issue in development. DES 1.6 'Landscaping and Trees in Development Schemes' provides an extensive criteria-based design policy split into eight sections addressing a range of hard and soft landscaping requirements, and their implementation. The policy highlights that landscape design should not merely be bolted on to a proposal as an afterthought, but needs careful consideration from the outset. Principles focus on landscape at a variety of scales and consider crime prevention and security as fundamental to a good development proposals.

An existing site survey will be required with the aim to protect existing trees. The survey typically acts as a constraints study and allows officers to assess the impact of a proposal, the intention being that all proposals contribute to a net improvement to the urban environment. Haringey acknowledge that landscape design can lead to the success or failure of a development. Policy DES 1.6 is therefore applied to all development within the borough and, alongside policy to protect the borough's open space, acts as Haringey's overarching policy on landscape.

Haringey, greening the street

Haringey: DES 1.6 Landscaping and Trees in Development Schemes

The Council will require developments to be appropriately landscaped to provide a suitable and pleasant setting for the proposed development, which integrates well by means of pedestrian and visual links with surrounding landscape features of natural or ecological interest. In those cases where landscaping is required, the following criteria should be taken into account:

1. Landscaping schemes should contribute to the street scene with space provided for this purpose.
   Schemes should include:
   - tree planting and protection of existing trees;
   - ground and shrub cover, hard surface and paving materials, grass verges;
   - adequate lighting and continuity of fencing or walling;
   - boundary treatments which reduce the likelihood of graffiti;
   - adherence to the principles of designing out crime;
   - landscaping of parking areas.

2. Requirements should be considered at the initial stage of the detailed application for an integrated landscape scheme which should be included at the design stage of any detailed application and not fitted in afterwards. All trees to be retained should be distinguished from new trees. Proposals for future maintenance should be included.

3. Consideration should be given to:
   - boundary planting to integrate the development with neighbouring sites;
   - the use of climbing plants against flank walls;
   - the provision of low shrubs to soften settings of buildings;
   - provision of amenity space.

4. Development proposals should, where possible, take advantage of opportunities for nature conservation and habitat creation, especially in intensely developed urban environments.

5. A site survey shall be submitted as part of the landscape scheme prior to approval, plotting all existing trees and shrubs, including height, spread and condition with existing and proposed levels and any trees and shrubs to be lost shown clearly.

6. Conditions on planning permissions will require retention and protection of trees of amenity value during construction and after the completion of the development. Plans should show the means of protection to be employed during construction. Details of site excavations may be required to be submitted and approved so that damage to roots and tree loss can be avoided.

7. Replacement or additional trees should be of a suitable size and species for the existing site conditions and should take into account other species growing in the area. Trees should be of a suitable species for the particular purpose for which they are being planted, i.e. whether for screening or enhancing the development.

8. Semi-mature trees should be planted where the setting of proposed buildings is particularly sensitive.

(Circular 11/95: The Use of Conditions in Planning Permission, offers model conditions for effective landscape implementation). Treating landscape (or detailed architectural design) considerations as reserved matters will rarely give such concerns the prominence they deserve in the planning process and may undermine their effective delivery.

Inset 34: Supporting innovative architecture

In **Leicester**, the decision has been taken to promote high quality modern design. Thus policy UD07 highlights the intention to encourage contemporary architecture and establishes the city's aim to deliver high quality architecture generally. Leicester's urban design team argue that this decision stems from the desire to make the city attractive as a place to live, work and invest, and that no dichotomy exists between securing contemporary architecture and high quality urban design.

Leicester, innovative architecture

The wording of the policy is concise and features a list of key design parameters — mass, scale, proportions, rhythm, order, unity and expression — against which judgements can be made. Although officers doubt that this policy has encouraged modern design in the past, they feel it establishes that applications will be judged on their merits (regardless of style) and that the city welcomes innovative proposals.

Further design policies progress this theme, with UD11, for example, dedicated to the design of corner buildings. The city recognises that corner buildings provide critical focal points and orientation devices and can aid legibility. The policy promotes the concept of getting 'design kicks out of corners' and establishes that such development is subject to additional requirements (see **Inset 57**). It reflects Leicester's comprehensive approach to urban design within the plan.

Leicester: UD07 High Quality and Modern Building Design

3.25 High quality environments and design enhance people's lives. There should be no conflict between high quality design and the construction of robust buildings that function well, are sustainable and meet the needs of their occupants and the occupants of the future. Individual expression and variety of architectural style is encouraged. It is recognized that in certain circumstances designs that contrast dramatically with adjoining buildings are highly desirable. The circumstances of individual locations will determine where this approach is appropriate. Buildings that are robust, flexible and are of high visual quality can help prolong the use of and life of buildings by being flexible and adaptable to change.

3.26 The City Council is committed to improving access for disabled people to the built environment. Developers will be expected to follow guidelines set out in SPG 'Paving the Way' in new development or refurbishment in the city. Developers also need to consider Policy AM01 in the Access and Movement Chapter that deals with pedestrians, people with limited mobility and new development.

UD07. HIGH QUALITY AND MODERN BUILDING DESIGN

High quality building design will be expected in all new development and will include consideration of the mass, scale, proportions, rhythm, order, unity and expression of proposed new buildings.

Planning permission will not be granted for poor quality or inappropriate design. High quality modern designs, whether they are interpretations of traditional styles or not, will be encouraged where they can demonstrate that the existing surroundings have been taken into consideration.

Inset 35: Design codes and the plan

Cotswold District Council emphasises the importance of good design through their Design Code. The code is written as supplementary design guidance to accompany the plan, and seeks both to cover the key aspects of architectural design and to set new standards for development in the district. Originally written to echo the Prince of Wales' ideas about the priority of harmony, local materials, and details and decoration, the code establishes what it calls the 'Cotswold Style' and stresses the importance of setting, streetscene, proportion, simplicity, and craftsmanship. Guidance notes within the plan state that 'the council will consider applications with reference to the Cotswold Design Code', while the code itself is essential reading for developers, architects, and builders.

The Cotswold
DESIGN CODE

Design coverage and presentation of the code provides a robust and functional piece of supplementary design guidance, which allows the council to argue for very high quality design improvements. The code covers the whole of the district and has been particularly useful in establishing the importance of good quality design outside of conservation areas. However, the blanket nature of its coverage has sometimes proved problematic as the district includes areas that have neither a tradition of the Cotswold style or the use of stone. These issues, coupled with the release of *By Design*, are necessitating some revision of the code.

Originally, the council intended the code to be included in the plan as a seven-point policy. Its removal from the May 1992 plan was based on the Government view at the time that such material made plans overprescriptive, overelaborate and slow to adopt. **Guildford** is pursuing a similar approach with the adoption of their ten-point design code policy. Positioned at the beginning of the plan to highlight its importance, the code is the first step in the consideration of a planning application. Guildford's intention is to avoid diluting the strength of their design policies by placing them in one location rather than spreading them throughout the plan. The code reinforces conservation in design and advocates a contextual, townscape-

Guildford: 99G2 Design Code

4.26 The Council gives a high priority to the protection and enhancement of the built environment. Each development proposal will be assessed in the light of the Design Code and those which conflict with the code will be rejected. Applicants should be able to demonstrate how they have taken account of good design in their development proposals.

99G2 Design Code
All development proposals will be expected to comply with the following design requirements:

99G2 (1) Context for Design
New development respects established street patterns, plot sizes, building lines, topography, established views, landmark buildings, roof treatment, aspect and other townscape elements.

99G2 (2) Scale, Proportion and Form
New buildings respect the scale, height and proportions and materials of the surrounding environment.

99G2 (3) Space Around Buildings
Existing spaces of value are respected and new spaces created though development should have an attractive and identifiable character.

99G2 (4) Street Level Design
Buildings and spaces at pedestrian level provide visual interest and a sense of place and identity.

99G2 (5) Layout
The built layout is easily understood by the user and creates areas of identifiable character.

99G2 (6) Public Views and Roofscape
Public views are protected and opportunities to create attractive new views and vistas are provided and encouraged.

99G2 (7) Materials and Architectural Detailing
Materials are of a high standard and harmonise with surrounding buildings. Detailing on new buildings is durable and reinforces the identity and character of an area.

99G2 (8) Traffic, Parking and Design
The visual impact of traffic and associated access and parking is minimised, especially in sensitive locations.

99G2 (9) Landscaping
A high standard of landscaping, to include walls, enclosures and paving schemes, as well as trees and other planting is provided to ensure that new development integrates into the existing townscape.

99G2 (10) Open Spaces of Value
Open spaces, whether public or private, which contribute to the character of an area, in terms of the views they create, the feeling of openness they allow, are protected.

dominated approach to development, and is seen as the guiding principle for all forms of development. At present, Guildford does not intend to convert the code to supplementary design guidance, and instead is working with other councils in Surrey to develop a 'Surrey Design Code'.

12. Policies should encourage the use of architectural skills and the development of contemporary designs that respect their surroundings

Architectural policies should be deliberately de-emphasised as part of a conscious effort to assert the importance of urban design concerns over matters of architectural aesthetics, and in a bid to get controllers, councillors and the public to shift their attention away from matters of design detail to more fundamental issues that affect the quality of built form and the public realm. That is not to deny the essential contribution that architecture can make to the quality of the urban and rural environment, but rather to focus authorities' attention on matters of landscape, site characteristics, siting, layout, the handling of vehicles, and the creation of public space.

It should be recognised both that architectural control is a highly controversial issue and that many controllers' understanding of architecture is often limited. The very existence of development control, let alone its practice, has sometimes contributed to a situation where 'safe' designs that tend to mimic their surroundings, or utilise a pastiche of architectural details, predominate. Such designs contribute just as surely to the destruction of local distinctiveness.

To counter these trends, policies should explicitly encourage contemporary designs that respect their context, but which make more imaginative use of the fundamentals of architecture — structure, technology, function, materials and visual interest (**Inset 34**). The key issues of context can often be encapsulated in questions of the scale, proportions and modelling of the façade, its vertical/horizontal emphasis, relation to urban grain and topography, its contribution to an interesting skyline and to patterns of landmark versus background architecture, and in the creation of active frontages at ground floor level and the use of appropriate materials (**Inset 35**).

CABE in a guide to their *Design Review* (2002) service argue that as regards architectural design: 'We believe that assessing quality is to a large extent an objective process. Ultimately, of course, some questions come down to matters of individual taste and preference. It is not often, however, that questions of this kind are important in deciding whether a project, judged in the round, is a good one. What matters is quality, not style'. The criteria they use to make judgements about architectural design reflect these broader concerns:

1. Order.
2. Clarity or organisation, from site planning to building planning.
3. Expression and representation.
4. Appropriateness of architectural ambition.
5. Integrity and honesty.
6. Architectural language.
7. Conformity and contrast.
8. Orientation, prospect and aspect.
9. Detailing and materials.
10. Structure, environmental services and energy use.
11. Flexibility and adaptability.
12. Sustainability.

In encouraging better architectural design, policy will implicitly encourage the better use of architectural skills. Explicit promotion in action plans of the value added by trained designers will also be useful.

13. Policies should encourage the coordination and positive management of the urban environment

Consistent with a broader view of design that strives for a general enhancement of environmental quality, policy should address issues of urban management and maintenance as well as small-scale private development. Although many of these concerns will be beyond a strict interpretation of the land-use planning remit (i.e. rubbish collection, graffiti removal, pavement maintenance, open space management, parking control, traffic calming, etc.), others will not and should be the subject of robust policy. The latter include:

- consideration of small-scale development issues, such as the use of security shutters, telecommunications apparatus, advertisement control, building alterations, extensions, replacement shopfronts, etc.;

Inset 36: A per cent for public art

Bristol, Leicester and Cheltenham all encourage provision of public art in development. Bristol's plan previously included a 'Per cent for Art' policy, now removed on the inspector's advice. The city is instead trying to resurrect the system through their planning obligation policy as part of a wider strategy to raise the importance of public art in development. This approach avoids the need for a fixed policy. Cheltenham employs a 'Council Action Policy' for public art. Policy GP A5 encourages the provision of art in development, but is dependent on council actions for delivery and is not enforceable on private developers (see Inset 37). Leicester's plan includes UD18 on public art which states that major developments will be expected to incorporate public art. Unlike Bristol and Cheltenham, Leicester establishes the delivery of art as a material consideration. The justification provides a criteria-based explanation of where UD18 is applicable, which is based on the scale of development.

Birmingham, public art in Centenary Square

Leicester: UD18 Public Art

3.54 The City Council will endeavour to provide art works and sculptures in the city. However, there is a growing awareness that much more could be done to improve the artistic quality of the built environment. One way of achieving this is by setting aside one percent of the capital budget for a new building or a major redevelopment for commissioning new works of art. The works of art could include detailed features on buildings, specially designed walls, railings, fencing, etc., and not just statues or sculptures. An improvement in the architectural quality of the building or its environment would also represent an artistic gain.

UD18. PUBLIC ART

Major development will be expected to incorporate public art. The determination of applications for planning permission for major development will have regard to the contribution made by any such works to the appearance of the scheme and the amenities of the area.

3.55 For the purposes of this policy a major residential development is one where the number of dwellings to be constructed is twenty-five or more or where site area is 1 ha or more. For all other uses a major development is one where the gross floorspace to be built is 1000 square metres or more, or the site is 1 ha or more.

- permitted development rights and, where appropriate, their withdrawal through the use of Article 4 Directions;
- hard landscape provision, including paving, boundary treatments, street furniture, signage and public art (see **Inset 36**); and
- applications for changes of use, particularly when impacting on ground floor frontages (see **Inset 31**).

In addition, planning departments through the coordination of their policy frameworks with other local authority departments, through their role in managing the planning process, and through their own enhancement proposals, can further influence the management and therefore quality of the urban environment (**Inset 37**). Examples include:

Inset 37: Council action policies on design advice

In **Cheltenham**, the local plan explicitly identifies actions the council will undertake as part of the planning process. Council Action General Policies do not apply to applications for planning permission. Rather they are statements of intent by the council itself. Policy coverage ranges from specialist design advice, to the preparation of supplementary planning guidance, to the seeking of informal environmental statements where appropriate. Different presentation in the plan, and identification as council action policies, is intended to differentiate them from development control policies and highlights that they are not a material consideration for planning. The intention is to inform an applicant of what action the council is undertaking and to create further transparency within the system. The impact of council action policies on design quality is unknown, although they do clearly establish what the council would like to see within a planning application, and encourage the submission of material that cannot be formally required by policy.

Cheltenham: Council Action GP A3

Design guides and development briefs

2.19 Advice on the form and design of development acceptable to the planning authority can be useful to all parties involved in the development process. In some cases, there is a clear 'right' and 'wrong', such as in new or replacement shop fronts (for which the Council has already adopted a design guide — see Council Action RT A70) or in alterations or additions to Regency buildings. Similarly, there are some aspects of new development where guidance can be particularly useful, such as protecting privacy in residential areas or designing to minimise crime. Suitable different design approaches not in specific accordance with the recommended solutions in a guide may still, however, be acceptable if to a sufficiently high standard.

2.20 PPG1 and PPG2 emphasise the Government's intention to work towards ensuring that development and growth are sustainable. They advise that local planning authorities should take account of the environment in its widest sense, including such new concepts as global warming and the consumption of non-renewable resources.

2.21 The Council's commitment to addressing wider environmental issues is stated in paragraph 1.61. It will seek to encourage the consideration of environmental issues in the development process and will produce design guidance to encourage building design and layout which enables the efficient use and conservation of energy resources and uses materials which are sustainably produced or recycled. The Council has already published an information leaflet on the use of tropical hardwoods.

2.22 Current design guidance has been published separately from the Plan, as Supplementary Planning Guidance. Its status is described in paragraph 1.16. During the Plan period, the Council proposes the publication of a number of other design guides, as resources permit, including:

- Designing for environmental sustainability
- Designing out crime
- Landscaping in new development (paragraph 5.50)
- Protecting and creating wildlife habitats (Council Action NE A46)
- Building extensions and alterations
- Street furniture and surfacing (Council Action BE A31)
- Industrial estate development (Council Action EM A57)
- Doors and windows to old buildings
- Porches, railings and walls
- Signs and advertisements

2.23 In some circumstances an individual site may merit a development brief to guide developers on matters such as building height, massing content, and other features.

COUNCIL ACTION GP A3
The Borough Council, in consultation with the public, will prepare and publish Supplementary Planning Guidance, and, in determining planning applications, will take account of such guidance as a material consideration. Where appropriate, the Borough Council will prepare development briefs for individual sites.

- their planning gain expectations and requirements, and the use of planning obligations;
- the use of planning conditions to planning permissions and the policing of their delivery;
- their procedures for requiring full or outline and reserved matters planning applications (including the system of certificates — 'Statements of Development Principles' — likely to replace outline permissions);
- the effort and resources put into enforcement processes;
- their shared policy stance and negotiations with the highways authority about road and footpath layout, design and specifications of details;
- enhancement provisions within conservation areas;
- more general plans for investment and enhancement of the public realm; and
- the consideration given to the design of the authority's own development proposals before consent is given.

Over time, the combined impact of small-scale development and local authority management processes makes a potentially significant contribution to the overall quality of the built environment. As major community concerns, such issues should be addressed in policy and, in particular, in the community strategy, which can be used as an opportunity to consider how the local authority will tackle cross-cutting interdepartment concerns, such as the management of the public realm, and how it will work with other interests outside the authority to better coordinate public and private sector investments (**Inset 38**).

Inset 38: Urban management and investment

Bristol has attempted to redefine the perception and pedestrian movement patterns in the city centre with its 'Legible City Initiative', through an integrated programme that addresses identity, transportation, information and art. The intention is to improve people's understanding, experience and enjoyment of the city. The initiative combines innovative principles with a flow of consistently designed information to provide the city with a clear visual identity, and to reinforce the character of individual neighbourhoods. The project is a major priority for Bristol City Council over the next decade, and is being developed by a wide ranging partnership of public and private stakeholders

The strategy intends to capitalise on Bristol's urban assets for the benefit of commerce, transport, culture, tourism and its people. Three key themes underpin the initiative — cohesion and integration, identity, and collective promotion. Each aims to reflect Bristol as a multifaceted and dynamic city. The programme avoids attempts to rebrand the city, and instead focuses on enhancing what already exists. Particular emphasis is placed on high-quality signage and information to improve legibility without creating visual clutter. An integrated arts programme is used to aid navigation of the city and provide positive landmarks. In essence, Bristol intends to create an easy to use, connected and enjoyable urban environment. Chapter eleven of the plan, dealing with the city centre, directly references the initiative and establishes legibility as a city-wide priority. Enhancement of city centre spaces and key pedestrian routes is also identified as playing a vital role in developing an 'accessible' city centre. Bristol's plan establishes a proactive approach to urban management, which is not just about delivering high quality new development, but is also about the way the existing environment is cared for.

Bristol, building a legible city

In the pursuit of the wider urban renaissance agenda such considerations should not be underestimated. As the Minister confirmed in September 2001: 'Maintaining and creating high quality public space has too often been pushed down the agenda, it's been squeezed by other priorities. We are determined to pull it up the agenda'. Planning (in partnership with a wide range of other stakeholders and local authority services) has a potentially decisive role in this and should be reflected in policy. The *Sustainable Communities* PPS encouraged such an approach, suggesting that: 'Ultimately the policies and proposals in a spatial plan must be linked to the achievement of social, economic and environmental objectives concerning the use and development of land. However, the policies may not all be entirely or directly expressed in land use terms' (para. 23). Nowhere is that broader vision for planning more important than in the pursuit of environmental quality.

Inset 39: Conservation policies in development plans

For the London Borough of **Wandsworth**, a primary UDP aim is the protection and enhancement of their townscape and built environment. Over 45% of the borough is designated with conservation area status and the district contains five historic parks and five commons. Conservation principles are viewed as fundamental to creating successful development, with policy focusing on a townscape approach. The plan highlights the importance of character, appearance and the urban grain of the particular area, while promoting development that respects any predominant styles of building. Wandsworth establishes that, where uniform design does not prevail, contemporary design of a high quality may be acceptable.

Guildford, like Wandsworth, promotes a dual approach to design and conservation. Policy aims to achieve conservation of the historic environment and supports new modern design where appropriate. Guildford's primary aim is not solely the protection of its historic townscape, but rather to maintain the borough's high quality environment for people who live and work there. As such, a balance is sought between conservation and contemporary design. Conservation policies extend to include locally listed buildings and advertisements, with an emphasis placed on development that responds to context and setting. Listed building and conservation area policy tackles development at a variety of scales, from the macro to micro, and is located in the historic environment chapter of the UDP. English Heritage previously identified Guildford's approach to conservation policy as a model of good practice, and policy has proven over time to deliver sensitive and responsive development within the borough.

14. Design criteria for conservation policies should be derived from conservation area assessments that emphasise design opportunities as well as constraints

Conservation area and listed building policies have generally been better developed in development plans than other design policies (**Inset 39**). It would appear that this is partly because central Government advice has long been well developed in this area (e.g. PPG15: Planning and the Historic Environment) and because English Heritage now provides a range of useful good practice notes. Conservation policies still need to be better integrated into design policies at large however, at both the district-wide and site-specific scales, and specifically need to incorporate urban design concerns (**Inset 40**).

In particular, it should be made clear that design policies are applicable everywhere, including in conservation areas, and that conservation contexts

Wandsworth: TBE24–TBE30 Conservation Areas

Policy TBE24 Proposals for new uses, development or demolition within conservation areas should preserve or enhance the character or appearance of the area. The policies in the Plan will be applied flexibly where this is necessary to ensure this.

Policy TBE25 Buildings which are in keeping with or contribute to the character or appearance of a conservation area and which are capable of further useful life should be retained wherever possible. Retention of original building structure and fabric will be sought.

Policy TBE26 The Council will normally require detailed applications for development in conservation areas, and proposals for demolition must be accompanied by details of proposed new development. Where appropriate, consent for demolition will be made conditional on implementation of an approved replacement development.

Policy TBE27 Development in conservation areas should respect the character, appearance, and grain of the particular area. It should respect any predominant style of buildings, but where a uniform design does not prevail, contemporary designs of a high quality may be acceptable.

Policy TBE28 The Council will prepare, undertake and promote enhancement schemes and other measures in conservation areas.

Policy TBE29 Article 4 Directions will be made, subject to confirmation by the Secretary of State where necessary, to control alterations harmful to conservation areas.

Policy TBE30 The Council will keep under review the designation of further conservation areas and extensions to conservation areas where it considers it desirable to preserve or enhance special character.

Wandsworth, A diverse conservation context

Guildford, A traditional conservation context

provide an opportunity for a more forceful application of the generic design principles. In this regard, the key consideration at all times should be context, and the contribution proposals make to preserving or enhancing its character and appearance. PPG15 indicates that of particular importance will be a detailed consideration of architectural principles including scale, height, materials, massing

Inset 40: Urban design in conservation contexts

The London Borough of **Haringey's** policies try to ensure that new development will not adversely affect the quality of the local environment. Their overall approach to design is conservation orientated and, in particular, aims to protect the character of the borough's terraced housing stock, which is increasingly being valued for its character. Thus an attempt is made to spread the concern for design and conservation issues across the borough and beyond its conservation areas alone. While the intention is to avoid a two-tier system of control, the UDP nevertheless provides eight policies focused on conservation areas.

DES 2.2 addresses the preservation and enhancement of conservation areas with the objective of reinforcing character. The policy addresses a variety of issues including demolition, new development, loss of amenity (including trees), repair of buildings and the general environment. DES 2.2 further highlights the townscape importance of local views, landmarks and topographical features. The policy goes on to describe council actions and intentions, regarding the preparation and publication of special guidance identifying local character and building types, and the undertaking of local environmental capacity studies. Prior to adoption, the inspector concluded that the design policies were too descriptive, and that many should be in supplementary planning guidance rather than in the plan. Some policies were also criticised for being too inflexible. Adopted policy now frequently uses the wording 'should' rather than 'must'.

Haringay, breaking down the volume

Haringey: DES 2.2 Preservation and Enhancement of Conservation Areas

The Council will seek to preserve and enhance the character and appearance of Conservation Areas and will normally refuse proposals within, adjacent to, or affecting a Conservation Area detrimental to the appearance, character or setting of the local area. The Council will prepare and publish special guidance identifying the local distinctiveness of areas, the types of buildings with Conservation Areas to be preserved and/or enhance and the weight to be given to the preservation or enhancement of these characteristics and features as against other development needs. The Council will:

1. Normally refuse applications which involve the demolition of buildings and structures which make a positive contribution to the character or appearance of the area and which define its identity.

2. Ensure high aesthetic design standards for all new build developments which respect and are sympathetic to the particular local character or appearance of the Conservation Area involved. New developments should have regard to the contribution to local character provided by (i) existing historic property plot sizes, (ii) traditional uses or mixes of uses, (iii) characteristic materials scaling of contemporary buildings and detailing, (iv) local views, (v) the extent to which traffic intrudes or reduces the enjoyment of an area by pedestrians, (vi) the intensity of development in the locality.

3. Resist the loss of trees which are of public amenity value and contribute to the character of the area.

4. Insist that changes of use, respect and enhance the local historic as well as visual character of the Conservation Area.

5. Protect local views, landmarks and topographical features, either within or adjacent to the Conservation Area, particularly key vehicular or pedestrian approaches, having regard to the policies and local views identified in DES 4.

6. Prepare and publish special guidance identifying the local character of areas and types of buildings within Conservation Areas to be protected and enhanced.

7. Enforce the carrying out of necessary repairs to unlisted or locally listed buildings in accordance with its powers when resources permit.

8. When resources permit, develop policies identifying local environmental capacity and programmes for enhancing the local environment including traffic management.

and alignment (para. 2.14) and with regard to respect for the patterns of street frontages, vertical or horizontal emphasis and fenestration will be particularly important (para. 4.18). In addition, it is important to consider the contribution patterns of established land uses make to the character of conservation areas, and, as English Heritage and the CABE have shown in *Building in Context, New Development in Historic Areas* (2001), that contemporary design can positively enhance the character and quality of conservation areas.

The main gap in conservation policy (and practice) appears to be the need to advance conservation area assessments as a means of both defining the key design considerations of relevance to control, and of identifying opportunity or neutral sites where redevelopment might enhance the character of the locality (**Inset 41**). The *Sustainable Communities* PPS explicitly identifies sensitive conservation contexts as suitable candidates for the production of action plans. Increasingly, English Heritage and others have also been emphasising the contribution conservation makes to achieving urban regeneration and sustainable development objectives. Integration with all these aspects of the policy agenda will also be important.

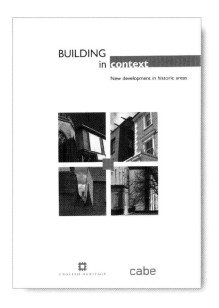

Inset 41: A checklist for assessing character (adapted from English Heritage, 1997)	
Issues	**Relevance**
1. Location and population	To set the area within the context of the wider settlement and to understand how the social profile of the area informs its character
2. Origins and development of the area	To establish how the area has grown and evolved, particularly to trace the morphological evolution of the area
3. The prevailing and former uses within the area	To understand how uses have moulded the character of an area, both as regards the form and layout of the buildings and spaces, but also regarding the social characteristics of the public realm
4. The archaeological significance of the area	Because expert assessment may be desirable to ensure proper regard is applied to underlying archaeology
5. The architectural and historic qualities of buildings	To make reference to any dominant architectural styles or building traditions, and any groups of buildings making a special contribution to the character or the contribution of the roofscape
6. The contribution made by unlisted buildings	To ensure that buildings without statutory protection in their own right are still recognised for the contribution (or detraction) they make to the area character
7. The character and relationship of spaces within the area	To ensure particular regard is given to the relationship between public and private space in an area, but also as a means to define townscape and visual characteristics of space (particularly means of enclosure) and the ways in which spaces function
8. Prevalent and traditional building materials, textures, colours and details	Because the detail on buildings, the floorscape and street furniture often provide so much of the visual interest in an area, and so makes a major contribution to establishing local distinctiveness
9. The contribution of green spaces, trees and other natural landscape features	To recognise the vital part the natural and man-made green environment makes to the character of urban areas, in parks and gardens and in other urban spaces
10. The setting of the area and relation to its surroundings	To have regard for the wider landscape/townscape context and particularly to the topography, views and vistas to any countryside or landmarks
11. The extent of loss, intrusion or damage to an area	Because negative features or significant threats will often have as great an impact on character as positive ones, and will need to be addressed in subsequent prescription
12. The existence of any neutral areas	To ensure that all opportunities for enhancement are recognised, including opportunities for contemporary design

15. Policies should encourage the preservation of listed buildings and pay special attention to the qualities identified in their listing, and to their settings

Façadist, replica and pastiche solutions should be discouraged except as a last resort, while contemporary designs in conservation areas (and alterations to listed buildings) should be encouraged providing they are sympathetic to their conservation context. Listed building policies now hinge around the concept of the 'optimum viable use' consistent with their historic character, but should also stress the presumption against demolition (as should conservation area policy) and the need to ensure that design interventions have regard to the listed characteristics. More policy emphasis also needs to be given to the setting of listed buildings (**Inset 42**).

Of particular value in relating historic building preservation to the local context is the publication of local lists of buildings of historic importance in policy. Although these will not carry the statutory protection of nationally listed buildings, they nevertheless help to define and preserve local distinctiveness, and can offer a statement of intent to add key local buildings to the statutory list as opportunities arise. Such lists should extend to valued contemporary structures as well as to their more historic counterparts.

Watch points

- **Build on and coordinate what policy/design guidance already exists.** Build on and adapt existing design policy and guidance, rather than starting from scratch and improve and integrate what already exists.
- **Prioritise urban design.** Too often policy is dominated by a concern for detailed design considerations and omits the more fundamental concerns of urban design. Concentrate on the latter.
- **Remember landscape helps make places.** Landscape design is too often an afterthought. Policy should prioritise a high quality landscape and ensure landscape considerations are dealt with as a fundamental component of planning applications.
- **Value open space.** High quality public and green open space is critical to creating an environmentally and socially sustainable built environment.
- **Architectural design will remain to some extent subjective.** Policy should restrict itself to key principles including encouraging contemporary design and innovation and sensitivity to context.
- **Beware of the limitations of planning but do not undervalue its potential.** Although many of the processes that create the urban environment are beyond the direct influence of land-use planning, planners remain in the best position to make the connections and to establish a vision for quality, and to coordinate actions affecting the public realm. This role should be articulated in policy.

Inset 42: New uses in listed buildings

The London Borough of **Camden** believes the best use for a historic building is the use it was designed for. Policy EN39 'Use of Listed Buildings' encourages this but, where it is not practicable, will consider a change of use that will preserve the building's historic and architectural features. While the expression of the policy has changed during the plan's development to strengthen its application, its essence has been retained through successive reviews. The current adopted UDP confirms that proposals that would

Camden, former piano factory, now offices

result in the loss of architectural features, obscure the original plan form, layout, structural integrity, or otherwise diminish the historic value of the building will be resisted.

Camden's approach establishes historic building policies as a key component of design policies at large, while acknowledging that unused historic buildings are detrimental to the built environment. Additional listed building policies include EN38 'Preservation of Listed Buildings', which highlights Camden's general presumption in favour of the preservation of listed buildings and EN40 'Restoration of Listed Buildings', which asserts that the council will seek the retention and repair of structural elements and other original features in listed buildings.

Camden: EN39 Use of Listed Buildings

EN39 The Council will seek to ensure that listed buildings are used for purposes which make a positive contribution to their fabric, interior, and setting. Proposals for the continued use of buildings for the purpose for which they were originally designed, or for the reversion to that use where it has been changed, will be particularly welcomed and, where possible, supported, provided this would not be in conflict with other policies of the Plan. Proposals that would result in the loss of architectural features, obscure the original plan form, layout, structural integrity or otherwise diminish the historic value of the building will be resisted.

4.84 The best use for a historic building is the use for which it was designed and wherever possible this original use should continue or be returned to if at all possible. The best way of securing the upkeep of historic buildings is to keep them in active use. This may, most often, be the original use but, when a building erected for a need which no longer exists becomes vacant, appropriate alternative uses will be considered to secure the survival of the building. In all cases, the Council will consider whether a proposed change of use and the subsequent alterations the new use may require will preserve the architectural or historic interest of the listed building. Planning permission will not normally be granted for a change of use that would conflict with other policies in the Plan, and preference will be given to any priority use, such as housing.

- **Conservation does not mean preservation.** Conservation of the built fabric is a dynamic activity that accepts change as long as the resultant proposals work with and enhance the established urban context.
- **Avoid two-tier approaches to urban design.** Urban and architectural design is not just important in sensitive locations. Policy should aspire to deliver design quality everywhere.
- **The present will soon be the past.** Today's modern architecture and urban design will eventually be part of our collective heritage. Seek development that reflects the time and place and that enhances local context.

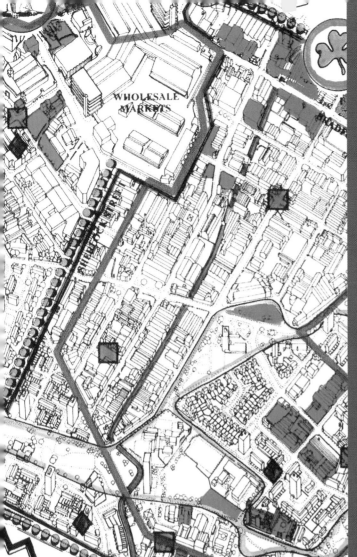

6

Writing, implementing and monitoring design policies

Writing, implementing and monitoring design policies

Preparing effective policies

The final set of recommendations move away from substantive design matters to deal with implementation and monitoring concerns, and with the relationship between adopted policy and other forms of non-statutory guidance.

The most carefully constructed policies will be of little value if the commitment to their implementation does not exist, but equally those responsible for implementing policy will be frustrated if the tools to address these objectives do not exist within the policy framework. This implies policies that deal with the full range of design issues that controllers face — particularly those that have caused difficulties in the past — and that are easy to understand and use, and capable of being defended at appeal. In essence, it means policies that are effective in meeting their objectives.

16. Policies should specifically respond to the most commonly encountered design problems and application inadequacies

Policies should respond to the most common design problems encountered in control and, where appropriate, carefully identify the key considerations enshrined in supplementary planning guidance. Such problems might include:

- those associated with householder applications — effects on neighbours, daylight/sunlight penetration, privacy, extensions and alterations;
- those associated with minor residential developments — conditions for infill/backland development, access, landscape, parking (**Inset 43**);
- or those associated with unsympathetic shopfronts and advertising.

Over-development is a common problem in city centres and other sought-after locations, although with the emphasis now on sustainable, compact cities, underdevelopment is being increasingly seen as a problem in suburban and centre/fringe locations. Central Government has emphasised (in PPG1 and in *By Design*) the importance of considering the scale, density, height and massing of development (para. A1) — all key aspects of three-dimensional building form. Policies controlling the amount of development on a site are critical to developers because they dictate the quantity of floorspace allowable and therefore the profitability of development. Therefore, such controls are always likely to be both the starting point and the flashpoint in negotiations.

Policy has generally moved away from reliance on various technical measures of acceptable densities across wide areas (largely plot ratio, habitable rooms per hectare, and daylighting controls) because of their inability to ensure that new urban forms respect the character of an area. In their place a variety of contextually-based criteria are required, such as adjacent building heights, massing, or the relation to established urban grain, to ensure the most appropriate level and

Inset 43: Controlling minor residential development

The London Borough of **Haringey's** policies are designed to preserve the character of the traditional housing stock of the borough, much of which is made up of terraced properties from the nineteenth and early twentieth centuries. The authority considers that minor details of existing houses make a great contribution to the character of residential areas and that many alterations carried out without planning permission as 'permitted development' have had a serious and adverse environmental impact. Policy DES 1.3 'Design of Alterations and Extensions' is extensive, and addresses a range of issues from the redesign of an entire façade to minor fixtures. Haringey believe that even the smallest details enhance the overall quality of the area and should be retained.

The overall approach is contextual and the policy is concerned with ensuring that minor development fits in with its surroundings. The policy justification suggests that all alterations and extensions should respect and be subordinate to the architectural character of the original building.

By such means the council intends to avoid minor development that disrupts the borough's townscape or architectural appearance. Officers believe that DES 1.3 has positively influenced the design of minor development and helped to retain areas of established environmental quality. In their conservation areas, policy is reinforced by detailed supplementary design guidance on architectural detail.

Haringey, controlling minor development

Haringey: DES 1.3 Design of Alterations and Extensions

Alterations and extensions should normally be in keeping with the plan, height, form, richness, architectural characteristics, style, period and detailing of the original building. Due regard should be given to established building lines, scale, setbacks, profile and silhouette. Existing finishes and features such as chimneys and porches should be preserved and extended using matching materials and colour.

1. Alterations and extensions should be confined to the rear or least important façades unless the result would sustain or improve the architectural character of the building in its setting; and any extension should be in scale with the building and the space around it.

2. In the case of alterations to the rear of a whole terrace, a new pattern may be set based on a traditional architectural character in keeping with the original buildings.

3. Additional or enlarged windows will be permitted providing that they do not harm the architectural integrity of the building, and that they follow the original pattern and materials.

4. Fixtures on buildings should be carefully chosen and sited to minimise visual impact.

5. Boundary walls and fencing alternations should have regard to the existing character of the area, the overall appearance of the proposal and the effect of the proposal on amenity, and should maintain adequate visibility for vehicles and not have an adverse impact on highway safety.

6. Balconies, roof terraces and external staircases should be in keeping with the elevational appearance of the building and locality, and should not cause serious problems of overlooking.

7. Basement excavations are generally not acceptable particularly where the residential density of the site would be excessively increased, where this would be visually intrusive or where this would conflict with the Council's residential conversion policies.

disposition of development. Nevertheless, as PPG3 emphasises (para. 58), minimum density requirements are still valuable to ensure the wise use of limited land resources and to encourage socially as well as environmentally sustainable development (**Inset 44**).

Inset 44: Dealing with density

The London Borough of **Camden's** plan has one of the most sophisticated standards-based approaches to density. Policy HG10 highlights the weight attached to density standards, as well as scheduling five circumstances where variations may be permitted. Circumstances for variation cover a variety of issues including townscape matters, conservation area designation, proximity to public transport, special needs housing, and proximity to open space (with the proviso that public open space or other leisure facilities will not be considered to be within easy walking distance if there are serious barriers to pedestrian access in the way).

In establishing its urban design-led approach to density, HG10 is cross-referenced and reinforced by DS2 'Residential Density Standards' in the 'Development Standards' section of the plan. DS2 establishes density zones within the borough related to three geographic areas (Hampstead and Highgate, central areas, and the rest of the borough), although with no obvious identification of where each area stops or starts. Standards are specified in both habitable rooms per acre and units per hectare with 'Family Housing' and 'Mixed or Non-Family Housing' differentiated. The expectation is that proposals should normally fall within the appropriate zonal range. To give maximum clarity to a policy otherwise likely to be contested, the plan provides definitions for density, habitable rooms and site area, and a useful calculation of density and a worked example of how site area (both net and gross) should be established.

Camden, residential density standard

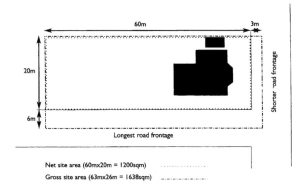

Net site area (60mx20m = 1200sqm)
Gross site area (63mx26m = 1638sqm)

Camden: HG10 Housing Density

HG10 Planning applications will be considered against the density standards set out in DS2 (chapter 16) and densities will be expected to be within the appropriate zonal range. Provided that satisfactory conditions for residents can be achieved in line with residential development and parking standards, variations to the range of densities specified in Development Standards may be permitted in the following circumstances:

a   where the need for compatibility with the existing character of the area and the scale and nature of adjoining development dictates a higher or lower density;

b   higher densities at locations within easy walking distance (400 metres or 10 minutes' walk) of public open space and other leisure facilities which provide adequate play and recreational opportunities;

c   in determining the scale of development in Conservation Areas, design policies or established local policies or guidelines will be used to dictate a higher or lower density;

d   higher densities in schemes providing predominantly special needs housing;

e   higher densities at locations within or close to Major and District Centres and public transport nodes.

6.42 When considering density, the objective will be the achievement of good quality housing in a satisfactory environment, with adequate amenity space. The boundaries of the density zones (A–C) are identified on the Proposals Map. Detailed guidance on the range, calculation and measurement of density is given in chapter 16. In each case, the density range has been drawn up so that the minimum is high enough to make the best use of housing sites in the Borough and the maximum low enough to ensure a satisfactory environment compatible with the site's surroundings. In defining the ranges and areas, the Council has taken account of the different character, accessibility and functions of areas in the Borough and the desire of some residents to live centrally at high densities. It is, however, necessary to assess each proposal according to the nature and location of the site, the character of the area and quality of the environment and the type of housing proposed. This may cause densities to vary not only from site to site but between areas. Variations to the range of densities may be appropriate in the circumstances identified above which are not exhaustive provided that satisfactory conditions for residents can be achieved in line with residential standards and parking standards. Guidance on appropriate densities for specific sites will be contained in planning briefs. In determining schemes for mixed uses which contain residential use, the Council's assessment will include the density of the residential element. Public open space or other leisure facilities will not be considered to be within easy walking distance of any point if there are serious barriers to pedestrian access such as main roads where there is no safe or convenient crossing point.

Inset 45: Criteria policies for urban design

In the City of **Westminster**, the UDP aims to clearly identify appropriate principles for development. Policy DES 1 is an overarching design policy for all development within the borough, which is criteria and process-based and positively worded. The policy was intended to reflect the increased Government emphasis on design in PPG 1 (1997) and *By Design*. Policy DES 1 is split into three sections addressing issues of architectural and urban design, amenity, mobility and community safety, and making planning applications.

Parts A and B are criteria based, with part A providing urban and architectural principles for development, and addressing townscape issues at a variety of scales. The approach taken is contextual, reflecting the high number of conservation areas and listed buildings within the city. Issues addressed range from sustainability, to the existing urban patterns of the area, to materials. Part B establishes design measures for safety, design against crime, and basic visual amenity. The final part effectively provides a checklist for applicants to ensure that they have taken into account an appropriate range of design concerns in their drawings and written statement. In a similar manner to **Richmond** and **Cheltenham** (see **Inset 12**), Westminster's DES 1 aims

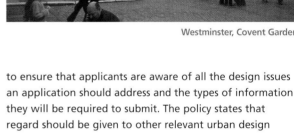

Westminster, Covent Garden

to ensure that applicants are aware of all the design issues an application should address and the types of information they will be required to submit. The policy states that regard should be given to other relevant urban design policies and supplementary design guidance. Officers believe that these design policies have consistently helped to deliver better design in the city.

Westminster: DES 1: Principles of Urban Design

Aim

10.6 To ensure the highest quality in the form and quality of new development in order to preserve or enhance the townscape of Westminster; to provide adequate access; to reduce crime and improve security.

POLICY DES 1: PRINCIPLES OF DEVELOPMENT

(A) Architectural Quality, Local Distinctiveness and Sustainability

Development should:
1. be of the highest standards of sustainable urban design and architectural quality;
2. improve the quality of adjacent spaces around or between buildings, showing careful attention to the definition, scale, use and surface treatment;
3. use high quality, durable and, where possible, indigenous and recycled materials appropriate to the building and its setting;

and should respect and, where necessary, maintain:
4. the character, urban grain, scale and hierarchy of existing buildings and;
5. the spaces between them;
6. the character, scale and pattern of historic squares, streets, lanes, mews and passageways;
7. the form, character and ecological value of parks, gardens and planned open spaces.

(B) Amenity, Mobility and Community Safety

To protect amenity, development should:
1. adopt appropriate design measures;
2. provide for safe and convenient access for all;
3. adopt design measures to reduce the opportunity for crime and anti-social behaviour;
4. where proposed, incorporate appropriately designed and positioned security fixtures on buildings and street furniture so as to minimise the visual impact of these fixtures;
5. maintain a clear distinction between private and public spaces around buildings and ensure the informal surveillance of public space.

(C) Applications

All development proposals should demonstrate how they have taken into account, by use of detailed drawings and a written statement, the following:
1. architectural quality, local character and distinctiveness;
2. the location and nature of existing and potential links to and through the site and to amenities beyond the site;
3. townscape features within the site and features which border the site;
4. local views through and within the site and landmark features visible in the vicinity of the site;
5. mobility and security measures;
6. regard to the relevant urban design policies contained in this chapter;
7. regard to supplementary design guidance produced by the City Council;
8. waste storage and disposal;
9. sustainable building principles in accordance with policy ENV 1: Sustainable and resource-efficient buildings.

17. Policies should be written with the means of implementation in mind — design consideration type policies are the most useful form of expression to achieve this

Policies should be expressed to make them directly useful to controllers and applicants. This means that vague 'motherhood' type policies of the 'there shall be a high standard of design' type (see **Inset 4**) should be avoided. Instead, authorities should try to define considerations or criteria by which applications will be judged. This injects greater precision into policies, reinforces a process-oriented conception of design, and encourages applicants to consider the full range of design issues while identifying those that are most relevant to the site.

Three particular kinds of policies can be identified which permit this:

- 'Consideration policies', which encourage designers to consider a range of factors when approaching a design problem without being unnecessarily prescriptive, and which provide the controller with a checklist against which to evaluate design outcomes.
- 'Criteria policies', which go a stage further and are a more precise statement of the criteria by which a planning application will be judged, while also avoiding the trap of being too prescriptive (**Inset 45**). Criteria policies are favoured in the *Sustainable Communities* PPS, but because it is difficult to be precise about the relevance of particular design qualities in every case, the term 'design consideration' is preferred here.

Inset 46: Clarifying policy expression

Development Plans, A Good Practice Guide published by the Department of the Environment in 1992 confirms that authorities should aim to offer 'guidance, incentive and control' through policy (para. 4.27):

- **Guidance**, to help people plan the use of their land confidently and sensibly, and to help planning authorities to interpret the public interest wisely and consistently. In design terms, if investment decisions are to be made with confidence and last minute disputes between applicants and authorities avoided, then enough guidance about design will be necessary to make requirements explicit without stifling design innovation and initiative, or overburdening the plan.
- **Incentive**, in that by allocating land for particular types of development in their statutory plans and supplementary guidance, local authorities may stimulate development activity. Indicating how individual developments relate to a broader vision can provide a significant incentive and confidence for development interests to invest.
- **Control**, which ensures that developers cannot ultimately insist on a development that is not in the public interest. For design, this implies clear policies robust enough to refuse planning permission on design grounds, and to defend that position with confidence at appeal. In design, as in other areas of the planning remit, the key legal tests can be applied: that policies should be necessary; relevant to planning; relevant to the development to be permitted; enforceable; precise; and reasonable in all other respects.

Inset 47: Selected glossary of design terms used in this guide

Sometimes a glossary can aid understanding. A selected glossary of the terms used in this guidance is offered as a means to encourage the consistent use and interpretation of key design terminology. A more comprehensive glossary is included in *By Design*.

- **Active frontages**: building frontages designed to display interior uses and activity to the adjacent streets and public space, either by extension of the activities into the space or by visual contact between, inside and out. Most commonly achieved by getting retail or commercial activity on the ground floor.

- **Area appraisal**: the systematic assessment of the design character and quality of a locality, embracing built and natural environment, social and physical character, land uses, and embodying public and design professional perceptions of the area.

- **Building envelope**: the three-dimensional external dimensions of a building — sometimes characterised as bulk.

- **Capital web**: the network of seen and unseen infrastructure that extends across urban areas and makes modern day life possible — services, roads, open space, transit networks, public facilities.

- **Character assessment**: a variant of area appraisal, but with a particular emphasis on historic characteristics and cultural associations for conservation purposes.

- **Cultural expression**: an expression of the varying cultural and ethnic identities of local populations in the built form.

- **Defensible space**: public space that is 'defensible' in that it is surveyed, demarcated or maintained by somebody.

- **Design briefs**: site-specific design guidance to supplement plan policy and to guide the design of development on a particular site.

- **Design frameworks**: define the three-dimensional form of public space over large areas, allowing individual developments to contribute to the development of a coherent public realm.

- **Design process**: recognises design as a 'process' and not just a 'product', in which a wide range of actors have important roles to play. The design process encompasses creative and analytical thought processes in a cyclical way, directed towards the resolution of disparate design criteria and constraints, to develop design solutions that can achieve widespread support and enhance localities.

- **Environmental capacity**: a measure of the carrying capacity of the environment (the amount of development the environment can absorb), before the natural systems operating in an area become distorted; it embraces measurements of the sensitivity of the existing environment and of the potential for new elements to positively strengthen attributes or to ameliorate impacts.

- **Form**: the shape of a building (architectural form) employed as a general concept to convey the visual character of buildings.

- **Human scale**: the scale of a building, space, or settlement that makes humans feel comfortable; related to the degree of enclosure and the proportions of buildings.

- **Landmark versus background architecture**: the visual significance of buildings in relation to others that determines if they stand out as landmarks or blend in as background. Traditionally, buildings of public importance are designed to stand out.

- **Legibility**: the quality that makes a place graspable (legible) and allows individuals to navigate around a settlement.

- **Local distinctiveness**: links people to locality by identifying what makes a place different from others and therefore special to its user; it incorporates concepts of identity, diversity, community, place and sustainability.

- **Massing**: the three-dimensional disposition of the different parts of the building, embracing height, bulk and silhouette.

- **Plot ratio**: a measurement of relative density calculated as gross floor area divided by net site area.

- **Public realm**: that part of the built environment to which the public have free access (streets, squares, parks, etc.); public realm issues embrace the social interaction and use of such spaces as well as their servicing and management.

- **Proportion**: the dimensional relation between one part of a building and another, and between one part and the whole.

- **Scale**: can be applied to architectural elements and compositions as well as to built forms and entire settlements. Architectural scale is principally determined by the relative size of the constituent parts of the building and by the modelling of the façade. The scale of built forms is principally related to urban grain, relative bulk, and enclosure.

- **Strategic design**: design beyond the microscale of architecture or single urban developments, to encompass the design of large areas of towns or cities or even whole settlements and their regions. It has regard to existing settlement patterns, patterns of growth, regeneration and infrastructure investment and to areas for conservation and containment.

- **Townscape**: the urban equivalent of landscape; what is perceived by the observer; or the 'art of relationship' created by weaving the physical elements of the city together to create visual drama.

- **Urban design strategies**: give spatial expression to urban design policy, usually across whole towns or cities, and provide a mechanism through which detailed briefs and frameworks can be generated. They focus on opportunities and constraints and indicate where direct public intervention and enhancement are required.

- **Urban form**: the overall three-dimensional form of a settlement and of the streets and spaces therein.

- **Urban grain**: the arrangement and size of the constituent parts of a town (the buildings, plots, blocks, urban spaces and building lines) that together determine the urban texture.

- **Vertical–horizontal emphasis**: the relationship between vertical and horizontal lines (indentations, projections, surface patterns) on the façade of a building.

- **Visual interest**: the extent to which the composition of a façade or space holds the eye, determined by the modelling, structure, fenestration, rhythms, skyline, decoration, floorscape, trees/planting, materials, colours, activities, public art, etc.

Inset 48: Designing policy documents

Gateshead, townscape

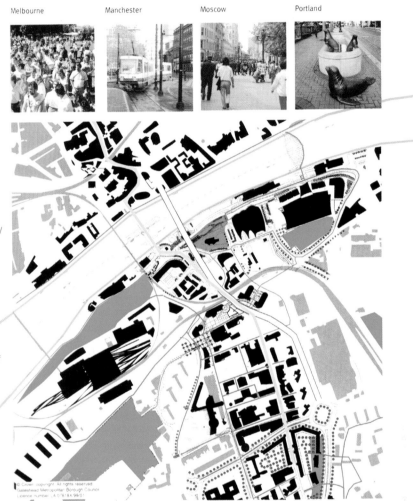

Melbourne   Manchester   Moscow   Portland

QUAYS TO TOWN CENTRE.

- Reclaiming the Quayside.
- Further development of the Sculpture Park.
- Creating linkages between public places and spaces.
- Riverside links - Swing Bridge/ Millennnium Bridge/ Tyne Bridge/ High-level Bridge.
- Dedicated Street Car - via Swing Bridge.
- Closing of East-West road between Tyne Bridge and High Level Bridge.
- Pedestrian routes between Town Centre and the Bridgeheads re-opened.
- Bottle Bank and old railway station area revitalised.
- New and safe pedestrian links to developments of Music Centre and Baltic Arts Centre.
- Formation of a new landscaped Gateshead Circus with pedestrians given priority of movement.
- Creation of a new Town Hall Square and a restoration of this former active urban area.
- Links between Town Hall Square and the Greenesfield site.
- New uses and restoration of existing buildings between Town and Greenesfield.

23

The nature of the plan and its quasi-legal status often restrict opportunities to design an attractive and accessible document. Council budgets also inhibit the creation of user friendly and attractive documentation, particularly at draft stage. In response, many authorities have invested in high quality supplementary design guidance that is more consumer focused and easier to use. **Westminster, Birmingham, Leicester, Cotswold, North Norfolk** and **Leeds** all produce well designed supplementary design guidance that helps to clearly explain design policy objectives.

Such guidance is able to use illustrative sketches, photographs of built examples and, in some cases, even schematic details.

As well as providing additional policy detail and explanation, the visual nature of these documents helps to avoid the need for extensive urban design jargon. Context appraisal is often provided in the form of historical and urban design analysis, while case studies are sometimes included, which further establish the level and quality of development required. By such means, increased development certainty can be achieved, since applicants are made visually aware of the design standards deemed appropriate by the council. The emphasis in the future on briefer policy frameworks and action plans should provide increased opportunities to learn from the presentational opportunities that currently only supplementary planning guidance seems to provide.

'Standards policies', which provide quantitative measures of certain qualities that are important to design quality (daylight, sunlight, amenity space, car parking). Used incorrectly, however, these may in themselves prevent more creative and contextually appropriate solutions. The better alternative is to define a set of performance standards which specify the qualities that should be achieved but not the physical quantity required.

Consideration and criteria policies allow designers to trade one issue off against another — an essential feature of good design. However, they should never be seen as rigid checklists to be ticked off by designers or controllers alike. Similarly, standards must never be viewed as ends in themselves, only as a means to help ensure high quality outcomes are delivered, i.e. as guidance. They should be used to encourage more sustainable outcomes, for example by reducing parking standards, and should always be closely related to local areas and contexts and not used as blanket prescriptions. The Government publication *Places, Streets and Movement* indicates how it is possible to move beyond standards-based approaches to road layout through the adoption of contextual design principles.

Inevitably, different forms of expression will suit different types of policy depending on whether the authority is attempting to guide, encourage or control particular types of development (**Inset 46**). Policy writers will need to consider the objectives of each policy carefully before deciding on the appropriate mode of expression. Complicating matters is the fact that design relies to some extent on its own terminology which, to remain accessible to lay readers, requires simplification and explanation. A glossary of terms is one solution (**Inset 47**). Expression should therefore use plain English (wherever possible), be positively phrased, and avoid the excessive use of referencing and footnotes. Policy text can also be reduced and simplified by the inclusion of illustrations, for example of key urban design principles. As a general principle, policy documents should be attractively illustrated (possibly with examples) and well designed in order to drive home key messages (**Inset 48**).

While ensuring their careful adaptation to the characteristics and priorities of the local context (authority-wide and/or sub-area), the economical approach to policy writing is likely to be intelligent plagiarism of design principles and policies from existing well-developed sources (other plans or design guidance or academic writing). This reflects the pattern of much recent policy writing activity.

Finally, it should never be forgotten that design policies need to reflect the priorities of the full range of user groups that engage with the planning process. They therefore need to be politically acceptable and comprehensible to the local authority members and the wider community, economically realistic for development interests, and flexible enough not to stifle the imagination of designers while allowing meaningful negotiation on development proposals. Striking the right balance is the essential art of the policy writer. The Planning Officers Society guide *Better Local Plans, A Guide to Writing Effective Policies* (1997) provides much more guidance on detailed policy writing concerns, as does *Making Plans, A Practical Guide* from the ODPM (2002).

Inset 49: Developing a hierarchy of design guidance

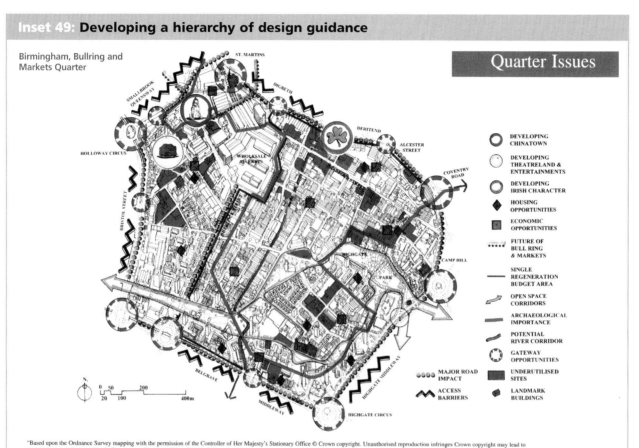

Birmingham, Bullring and Markets Quarter

Quarter Issues

- DEVELOPING CHINATOWN
- DEVELOPING THEATRELAND & ENTERTAINMENTS
- DEVELOPING IRISH CHARACTER
- HOUSING OPPORTUNITIES
- ECONOMIC OPPORTUNITIES
- FUTURE OF BULL RING & MARKETS
- SINGLE REGENERATION BUDGET AREA
- OPEN SPACE CORRIDORS
- ARCHAEOLOGICAL IMPORTANCE
- POTENTIAL RIVER CORRIDOR
- GATEWAY OPPORTUNITIES
- MAJOR ROAD IMPACT
- UNDERUTILISED SITES
- ACCESS BARRIERS
- LANDMARK BUILDINGS

"Based upon the Ordnance Survey mapping with the permission of the Controller of Her Majesty's Stationary Office © Crown copyright. Unauthorised reproduction infringes Crown copyright may lead to prosecution or civil proceedings". Birmingham City Council LA 076104 1996.

Birmingham has a hierarchical approach to design policies. Part one of the plan establishes citywide policies that set out a framework for managing change within the city, with design policies primarily located in Chapter 3 'The Environment'. Part two provides area-specific design guidance for each of Birmingham's constituencies in the form of concise continuous statements of policies and proposals. These effectively address how the overall strategy and policies (including design) will be applied to particular places. The UDP then provides the framework for a number of tiers of supplementary design guidance, and cross-references in each case the various pieces of planning guidance that may be relevant.

City-wide supplementary design guidance includes 'Places for All' and 'Places for Living' (see **Inset 58**). The city centre is covered by a series of Quarter Frameworks, including the Convention Centre Quarter, the Jewellery Quarter, the Gun Quarter, the Digbeth Quarter, the Bullring and Markets Quarter, and the Lee Bank Estate Plan. These studies were born out of Birmingham's earlier City Centre Urban Design Study (BUDS), which is now being taken forward in a second generation of city-wide and sub-area guidance down to the level of site-specific planning and design briefs.

Birmingham's current plan is an alteration to the earlier adopted plan rather than a completely new document. Officers believe the latest plan addresses design issues more comprehensively and will necessitate more supplementary design guidance to deliver its key provisions. These will be viewed as extensions to the plan, rather than as stand-alone policy frameworks. Most documentation is produced in-house, although specialist consultants have sometimes been employed. The ability to produce comprehensive urban design information nevertheless reflects the authority's decision in the late 1980s to appoint urban designers to work alongside mainstream planning staff in integrated cross-professional teams. Birmingham views this as a major innovation in their planning processes.

Birmingham's approach to policy has for some time placed a considerable emphasis on supplementary planning guidance and, in light of policy changes in the Planning Green Paper, it is expected that this emphasis will increase. Other design-aware authorities such as **Leicester** (see **Inset 8**) and **Stratford-on-Avon** (see **Inset 52**) are emulating the approach.

18. Area and site-specific guidance should be organised hierarchically, cross-referenced to authority-wide design policy, and preferably adopted in the local development framework

Among the most effective implementation mechanisms will be the preparation of additional design guidance on an area or site-specific basis — detailed information on the preparation of which is available in *By Design* and *Urban Design Guidance: Urban Design Frameworks, Development Briefs and Master Plans* from the Urban Design Group (2002). Development plans have been able to act as the statutory framework for all manner of supplementary design guidance — area appraisals, conservation area assessments, regeneration strategies, urban design frameworks, area-wide design guidance, site-specific design briefs and three-dimensional master plans (**Inset 49**). Far too often, however, no reference is made to any of these documents, and they are assumed to have a *raison d'être* of their own, divorced from statutory policy.

It should never be forgotten that only those policies that appear as adopted policy carry the extra weight imbued by the plan-led system (Section 54A of the 1990 Town and Country Planning Act). Therefore, like any other area of planning, a comprehensive range of design policies should benefit from those provisions. Significantly, the 2001 Planning Green Paper proposed major changes to plan making in England, and envisaged many of these supplementary forms of guidance being formally adopted as part of the LDF, many as action plans. Thus the local development framework might include guidance for particular areas or sites (including development briefs, guidelines and master plans), neighbourhood, village and area plans, and even topic-based guidance for larger areas or particular issues such as residential design. Although some of this guidance may not be formally adopted and therefore remain non-statutory — at least in the short-term — the *Sustainable Communities* PPS made it clear that such design guidance should still be incorporated into the local development framework.

The relative balance between what is formally adopted and what remains as non-statutory guidance will therefore become a matter for local consideration. Adopted policies and non-statutory guidance will nevertheless also benefit from being organised in a hierarchical way to create a logical relationship between each, and to improve their comprehension and application. As a long-term objective, the core strategy in the LDF should be elaborated through an authority-wide design statement (see Chapter 3), and a hierarchy of action plans in the form of urban design frameworks/master plans, other area design strategies/plans/statements, development briefs and so forth. The more the different levels of guidance are cross-referenced to each other, and preferably collated in the LDF, the stronger their educative and operational value to applicants, controllers and the general public. **Inset 50** indicates how the new hierarchy of design guidance relates to that which it replaces.

Inset 50: The design policy hierarchy — new and old

Old hierarchy	Role and utility		New hierarchy
National guidance			
1. **Primary legislation** (planning Acts)	Provides the statutory basis for planning and conservation, and therefore for development and design control.		1. **Primary legislation** (planning Acts)
2. **Planning Policy Guidance (PPG)**	Sets out Government policy on planning matters, including design, with a new stress on urban design. Lays down the limits of design as a material consideration, thus limiting local choice. Such guidance is a paramount material consideration, but remains general and flexible in nature requiring interpretation in the light of local circumstances.	Will gradually replace PPGs and, in so doing, set out Government policy on planning matters in a more clear, concise and focused manner. Will focus on implementation of national objectives, but will focus on policy. Will remain the foremost material consideration in writing policy and making planning decisions.	2. **Planning Policy Statements (PPS)**
3. **Government advice** Circulars Design Bulletins Good Practice Guides	Gives Government advice on more detailed and technical design concerns such as crime or road layout. Criticism has been levelled over the tendency to encourage copycat solutions, and lack of interpretation in the light of local circumstances, i.e. DB32. More recently a sequence of good practice guides have articulated government aspirations on design more fully, i.e. *By Design, Better Places to Live, Places, Streets and Movement*.		3. **Government Advice** Circulars Design Bulletins Good Practice Guides
Strategic guidance			
4. **Regional Planning Guidance (RPG)**	Establishes broad regional emphasis on environment/design /conservation in the light of competing claims on resources. They have tended to ignore design as a detailed concern, at least until recent guidance, i.e. RPG9 'South East'.	Will have statutory status as the new strategic guidance under which local development frameworks and local transport plans should be prepared. Will be slimmed down from RPGs, but should establish environmental quality objectives.	4. **Regional Spatial Strategies (RSS)**
5. **Structure Plan/UDP Part 1 Policy**	Provides an opportunity (usually missed) to set out a spatial design/environmental framework to guide local plan policies, and to ensure the consistent emphasis of design and environmental considerations across district boundaries.	Will be prepared in some areas only as part of the RSS, i.e. where administrative boundaries would otherwise prevent proper planning. Like RSSs they will provide an early opportunity to establish the quality thresholds for development.	5. **Sub-regional strategies**
6. **Landscape Character Assessment**	Ensures emphasis is given to landscape concerns and helps ensure proper regard is had to natural environment design issues as well as to those concerning the built environment. Such appraisals are of maximum value if able to inform policy (prescriptive rather than descriptive).		6. **Landscape Character Assessment**
7. **County Design Guides**	Influential over the years particularly for residential development, i.e. Essex, Cheshire, Kent, Sussex guides. Ensures a consistent approach to design across districts. Tends to focus on county matters such as road hierarchy and broad vernacular, but they provide an opportunity to establish broad urban design principles, i.e. Essex. General at best, and no substitute for district policy.		7. **County Design Guides**
Authority-wide guidance			
8. **Community strategy**	Provides the opportunity to establish a community vision and aspirations, and to coordinate local authority services and actions towards securing more sustainable patterns of development.		8. **Community strategy**
9. **Local Plan/UDP Part 2 Policy**	Provides the most potent tool in the planning authorities armoury, benefiting from the full force of Section 54A of the 1990 Planning Act. Should be used to lay down a contextually relevant framework for design control. Closely scrutinised by central Government to prevent over-prescription. They include Generic Policies, as well as site-specific polices and proposals.	Develops the vision in the community strategy for land use planning and provides a concise statement of policy across all areas of the planning remit, including design. The local development framework carries the same weight as development plans in a plan-led system and the core strategy provides a framework for more detailed action plans. Site-specific polices are included in the proposals section.	9. **Local development framework — core strategy and proposals section**
10. **Authority-wide supplementary planning guidance (SPG)**	Sits outside of the plan and is therefore not subject to the status and provisions of Section 54A of the 1990 Planning Act. It nevertheless represents an important material consideration in the making of planning decisions. Government guidance advises that all key concerns that form the basis for decision making should nevertheless be formally adopted in the development plan.	Has the potential to incorporate all previous authority-wide supplementary guidance as an adopted part of the local development framework. Suitable for establishing design principles for particular types of development, but also to establish a robust and comprehensive set of authority-wide design policies expanding on the principles in the LDF core statement of policies. May also remain non-statutory (not adopted).	10. **Local development framework — authority-wide design statement**
	Design guides: Can be used to elucidate and disseminate design advice and to educate applicants, councillors and development controllers. Well suited to single design issues, or to different development types and contexts. They have the potential to develop urban design policy and to establish expected design standards with illustrated examples of best practice.		
	Design standards: Largely relate to residential amenity considerations (health and safety concerns) and to residential roads. Such quantitative measures rarely secure good design by themselves, and need to be operated flexibly and with skill, alongside other urban form policy to avoid over-regimented solutions.		
	Design strategy: Give spatial expression to urban design policy, and provide a mechanism through which detailed briefs and frameworks can be generated, i.e. the Birmingham Urban Design Study. A proactive form of guidance, best suited to expressing broad urban design issues and planned interventions in the urban fabric. They represent a major investment of resources in urban design and require an agreed vision of future form.		
	Landscape strategy: Focuses on managing and enhancing, as well as protecting landscape (urban and rural). Such strategies help integrate natural and built environment concerns, ensuring a more sustainable approach to urban design, for example *Cherishing Outdoor Spaces, A Landscape Strategy for Bath*.		
Area or site-specific guidance			
11. **Area/site-specific supplementary planning guidance (SPG)**	Sits outside of the plan and is therefore not subject to the status and provisions of Section 54A of the 1990 Planning Act. It nevertheless represents an important material consideration in the making of planning decisions. Government guidance advises that all key concerns that form the basis for decision-making should be a formally adopted plan in the development plan.	Potentially includes all previous area or site-specific supplementary planning guidance. These are proactive documents most likely establishing a design strategy for areas of change, but also appropriate in areas of conservation. They can be formally adopted as part of the local development framework or can remain non-statutory. They relate to local areas or sites.	11. **Local development framework — area action plans (and other statuatory SPG)**
	Area appraisal: Although resource intensive to prepare, area appraisal should form an essential part of the design policy writing process, ensuring that proper regard is given to the visual, social, functional and environmental context. It is vital to make appraisal analytical rather than purely descriptive, and to publish it alongside policy as a material consideration. Appraisals include conservation area assessments.		
	Design codes: Area related (but not site specific) urban design codes are usually used to guide the form of comprehensive development over long periods, often alongside a master plan. They can borrow cues from the surrounding context or define a new context, but do not by themselves provide certainty over the eventual urban structure, though developers can adopt them. They also require long-term will to implement, for example the *Guide to Development in Hulme, Manchester*.		
	Development/design frameworks: Proactive approach to encouraging an appropriate infrastructure and urban form on large, long-term development sites — roads, public transport, landscape and open space, nodes, connections, vistas, etc. Allows flexibility for designers to design within a coordinated controlling framework, and can be used to coordinate individual development briefs.		
	Master plans: Three-dimensional vision of future form (allowing architectural freedom within limits of defined form). They maximise certainty, but can reduce flexibility if too prescriptive. Their great advantage is their role in articulating a vision and ensuring appropriate relationships are created between built form and public spaces.		
	Development briefs: Proactive, readily adaptable, resource efficient guidance, well suited to defining the urban design, development and planning (not architectural) requirements of individual sites. Can be used to aid policy implementation, consultation, marketing and to lever planning gain. In practice they are too often ignored and lack design content, but nevertheless represent a material consideration and are capable of ensuring the best possible use of land and promoting design quality.		

19. Design policies should be systematically implemented through appropriately skilled development control processes that allow adequate time for negotiation

Fundamentally, authorities may have very high quality design policies, but if they are ignored or inappropriately used in development control negotiations, then their impact will be minimal. Therefore, as well as considering implementation in the wording of policies (i.e. how they are to be used), and writing policies and guidance frameworks that in themselves are creative and proactive, it is necessary to develop an appropriately design-skilled control team that systematically considers the design quality of the final outputs for every planning application received.

This will require the retention of specialist design skills, but also a much deeper understanding of design across generalist planning staff about design. This matter needs to be addressed on several fronts. Ideally it would include establishing or appointing an urban design team or unit in order to negotiate applications and prepare the new forms of proactive policy and guidance (**Inset 51**). It should also include mechanisms for sharing policy monitoring information in order to educate

---

Inset 51: Design issues and development control

In **North Norfolk** the planning authority has been able to develop a system of design control — over a considerable period of time — based on negotiation and prescription by a skilled design team that has created a local 'design culture'. Applicants, agents and developers all now clearly understand that designs will need to reach a minimum standard before they can be accepted for approval. In such matters, the *North Norfolk Design Guide* has formed the basis for negotiation, which has been refined since its original publication in 1974 based on experience gained through development control practice. It is now adopted as part of the North Norfolk Local Plan.

A conservation and design manager has responsibility throughout the district for the conservation areas and historic buildings, and for the appropriate design of all new development. Thus, unlike many authorities where design negotiation is dominated by development control staff with little design training, and with occasional reference to a (usually) lone designer for advice, all proposals are submitted to a team of design professionals for consideration. Applications are viewed upon receipt and those failing to come up to the standard set by the guide are marked for latter action. The design team is subsequently consulted on the applications identified using the same administrative process as that for other consultees. The development control team negotiate simple

changes, with more complex negotiations handled direct by the design team. The design team is then involved at every stage of the development control process.

Wherever possible, prior informal discussions will also have taken place before an application is made. The intention is to provide a cost-effective means to avoid protracted negotiation from entrenched positions once the development control clock is ticking. In all this, the relationship between the design and development control officer is a crucial one, with care taken to ensure that quality in the built environment remains a key objective shared by all. Statistical analysis of the rates of processing planning applications in the district has indicated that the design negotiations procedure does not prolong the process of the application overall.

North Norfolk, principles for
new residential estates

Inset 52: Educating through design guidance

Stratford-on-Avon has been fostering an active and integrated approach to design guidance. The numerous Village Design Statements complement the *District Design Guide* and a poster format Countryside Design Summary, all of which have been adopted as Supplementary Planning Guidance. A principal aim of the guidance is to encourage design learning from existing settlements. The effort to improve design includes both internal and external sessions to actively raise the knowledge base of council members and development control staff, and to bring developers on board. At the level of individual settlements and parish councils, the VDS process has helped to build knowledge and increase local capacity for positive contributions to the development control process. While the authority believes the guidance plays a potentially significant role in facilitating the development control process, by laying out its expectations and highlighting cost implications to developers, they also acknowledge the need to constantly refer to the guide in discussions with applicants. The availability of a full-time urban design officer has been fundamental in securing more creative

solutions to development proposals, not least in helping to educate members and other officers. One such creative solution, resting on a design-led approach, resulted in the approval of a prominent development where the number of homes provided was increased from 100 to 160 units.

Stratford-on-Avon, streets within a settlement

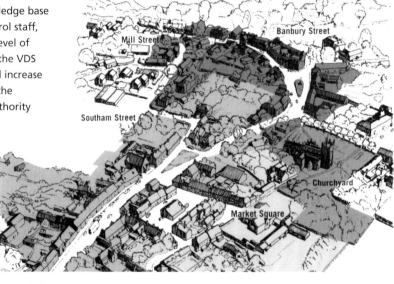

development controllers and councillors about their effectiveness (**Inset 52**). The urgency of this work was confirmed in 2001 when the then Minister convened an Urban Design Skills Working Group to consider the problem. It concluded that not enough local authorities have properly staffed in-house design teams and, as a result, the communities they represent were missing out on considerable economic, social and environmental benefits that the delivery of better quality development can bring (see **Inset 57**).

Raising design standards can be a time-consuming process, and any allocation of resources to deliver better design outcomes implies allowing more time for design (for example, time for pre-application negotiations). The move from eight-week statutory determination periods for planning permissions to 13 weeks (at least in the case of larger, more complex applications) is a significant help in this regard. The extra time should be used positively to ensure that the very best design outcomes are secured in all developments — both large and small.

At the same time it is important to recognise that design control is not some 'other' extra process that planning applications need to go through, but is instead something integral to development control decision-making. A concern for better

design should therefore be built into every stage of the development control process from pre-application to appeal (**Inset 53**).

Implementation can be enhanced through other mechanisms such as:

- ensuring adequate time is given over to pre-application discussions and negotiation;
- encouraging the involvement of different user groups in developing a design strategy and in writing policies;
- the use of inter-professional 'Development Team' approaches for major projects;

Inset 53: Design and the development control process

Before an application for planning permission is received
1. If necessary, instigate the preparation of an action plan — development briefing procedures or area guidance, or request the applicant to prepare appropriate guidance.
2. If appropriate, instigate a design competition, particularly for council-owned land.
3. If appropriate, instigate collaborative and participative arrangements.
4. If development interest, offer the means for potential developers to consult the authority about design proposals.

After an application for planning permission is received
1. Appraise the site and its surroundings to establish the design context.
2. Review established design policies for the site (existing sources of design policy and guidance — national/regional/authority-wide/area and site specific).
3. Review the application to ensure design aspects have been clearly, appropriately and accurately presented (drawings to include context analysis, three-dimensional representations, development in context, and a design statement as appropriate).
4. Instigate public consultation procedures.
5. Obtain skilled/specialist advice (i.e. Design review panel procedures, historic building specialist, landscape specialists, CABE, English Heritage, etc.).
6. On the basis of information gathered/received, negotiate design improvements.
7. Negotiate with other key public sector players, for example the highways authority.
8. Consider and negotiate implementation requirements (phasing, planning gain requirements, reserved matters, etc.).
9. On the basis of information gathered/received, prepare a report and make a reasoned recommendation or decision (grant permission, refuse permission, grant permission with conditions, grant with clearly defined reserved matters, defer and renegotiate).
10. If appropriate, invite the designer/developer to present their scheme to the planning committee.

After a negative decision has been made
1. If appropriate, invite the designer/developer to discuss and renegotiate and to seek alternative skilled advice.
2. Where necessary use the information gathered/received to fight any appeal.
3. Use the appeal decision to monitor review procedures, but also — where necessary — to revise design policy and guidance.

After a positive decision has been made (or an appeal successfully made)
1. Carefully monitor the implementation of all aspects of the design (and if necessary negotiate and/or enforce decisions/conditions/reserved matters).
2. Evaluate the final design outcomes on the ground.
3. Use the information to monitor review procedures, but also — where necessary — to revise design policy and guidance.

- proactive initiatives like promoting design award schemes or establishing local design panels; and
- encouraging increased planning officer and councillor design awareness through continuing professional development (CPD) activity.

Many such initiatives are discussed in the context of planning for housing in *Working Together, A Guide for Planners and Housing Providers* (Carmona *et al.*, 2002). In addition, the Planning Officers' Society guidance *Moving Towards Excellence in Urban Design and Conservation* (1999) offers much useful guidance on managing a design and conservation service in the light of the 'Best Value' regime and the drive for service improvement across local government (see below). Finally, as PPG1 emphasises (para. A6), the wise use of conditions to planning permissions and planning obligations can also be useful in helping to secure better quality design.

20. Design policies should be systematically monitored to assess and improve their effectiveness, and to ensure political and public support for design control

While the recommendations so far have identified a wide range of potential policies and various ways of writing and organising them, it is not envisaged that any plan will attempt to take all these suggestions onboard at once. Rather, the intention is to encourage a critical appraisal of existing policies, and a periodic but profound debate between councillors, controllers, policy writers and the public on their content and focus.

Today, many plans have a relatively new set of policies that have often not been fully evaluated by either policy or control sections, or by local politicians. Now that the majority of local planning authorities have adopted their district-wide development plans, the next task is to monitor carefully the utility of these policies in improving the design quality of applications and in conducting negotiations on design matters. The aim should be to identify the gaps in policy coverage and loopholes in policy wording as a basis for preparing LDF core strategies and action plans.

Unfortunately, the monitoring of design policies remains almost non-existent. If policies are to be progressively improved (made more effective) and control skills better developed, then monitoring needs to be given much more attention and preferably built into the wording of policy from the start. Monitoring provides an important mechanism for harnessing political and public support by demonstrating the 'value added' by local authorities improving design.

Partly because of their origins in the Local Agenda 21 Plans produced by local authorities, many community strategies are building in targets and indicators of their success from the start (**Inset 54**). This represents a valuable discipline for measuring the ongoing success of policies that should be more widely emulated in planning policy. It also reflects the messages coming through the 'Modernising Local Government' agenda and 'Best Value' regime, with authorities encouraged to adopt their own local indicators of success across all policy areas — including environmental quality.

The Planning Officers' Society guidance *Moving Towards Excellence in Urban Design and Conservation* provides a valuable start, by recommending a wide range of performance measurement targets and monitoring systems against ten critical factors for an excellent design service:

1.   Focus on quality outcomes — stewardship (of the whole environment).
2.   Focus on quality outcomes — clarity of expectations (in policy and guidance).
3.   Focus on quality outcomes — consistency of decisions (based on clear criteria).
4.   Focus on quality — ensuring compliance (with decisions through enforcement).
5.   An integrated service (with other 'environmental' services).
6.   A well-resourced service (with knowledgeable and committed staff).
7.   A well-managed service (proactively managed within the planning process).
8.   An influential service (promoting the key strategic objective of quality).
9.   An accessible service (available to all and reaching out to users).
10. A user-focused service (engaging the support of all stakeholders).

Inset 54: Setting targets for action

Both the London Borough of **Camden** and **Salford** have gone through a process of partnership creation and consultation to develop their community strategies. In both cases, in order to monitor the implementation of the strategies over time, a range of specific targets are established under each key strategic theme (96 in Camden and 55 in Salford). Each authority aims to produce annual action plans to set out new targets and identify how they will be met. Camden's first action plan systematically describes each target and identifies:

■ when the target will be met;
■ who will take the lead in that process;
■ who else will be involved;
■ what actions will be required to meet the target;
■ what resources will be required to achieve the target;
■ how progress will be monitored; and
■ how success will be demonstrated.

For Target 74 on the better design and management of streets, for example, key responsibility falls with the Director of Environment, aided by the police, businesses, local community, public utilities and leisure and housing departments. By 2005 the authority aims to develop new processes for urban management, including reducing street clutter and investing in infrastructure. The capital programme will meet some of the resources required with the rest derived through more joined-up public/private working. Progress will be monitored by a range of methods including customer satisfaction surveys, analysis of the quality of finished work, and claims made about trips. Success will be demonstrated when satisfaction ratings of over 70% are achieved and the external auditor's reports are favourable.

COMMUNITY PLAN

OUR VISION FOR SALFORD
2001 - 2006

Monitoring of design appeals is particularly important, both to improve appeal proofs but also to amend policy in the light of central Government interpretations. Monitoring might also include some objective assessments of design outcomes through the evaluation of completed schemes with the planning committee, local professionals and the wider public, particularly those with a special interest in amenity (**Inset 55**). Properly constructed, systematic monitoring can almost be a substitute for area appraisal (see **Inset 15**), identifying the nature of environmental change and public responses to it, and assessing whether the current responses are adequate or in need of refinement (**Inset 56**).

Inset 55: **Monitoring design — a 'critical friend'**

The London Borough of **Richmond's** environment planning and review team, in conjunction with development control, is responsible for design monitoring within the borough. The authority is seeking to achieve 'Beacon Status' in urban design and is proposing a continuous audit on design, as recommended in *By Design*. The audit will be undertaken by what Richmond call a 'critical friend' who will be responsible for keeping a watching brief on design issues. This external consultant will assess Richmond's design approach at regular intervals, and recommendations will be fed back into the borough's multidisciplinary urban design team. Monitoring of sustainable design aspects of development is also proposed through a 'Sustainable Design Checklist'. The aim is to include the checklist with each set of planning application forms sent out in order to monitor the relative sustainability of development actually delivered in the borough.

Design monitoring is complemented by Richmond's 'Sustainable Design Award' scheme, intended to highlight the benefits of good design. Monitoring of committee member design skills is also undertaken with the borough providing design seminars for councillors as and when required. Richmond still see development control implementation experience as the primary influence on design policy writing, but view additional monitoring as highly beneficial, not least to ensure that previous experience gets properly fed back into the policy writing and development control processes.

Richmond Upon Thames, new housing in Twickenham
(Photo: Clive Chapman Architects)

Watch points

- **Avoid blanket density standards.** Density standards should be related to distinct character zones, which should be spatially mapped in policy.
- **Address different scales of development.** The quality of the environment is determined by the many small-scale developments, as well as by the far fewer number of major interventions. Policy should address the design requirements of each.
- **Justify standards.** Any standards need careful explanation and justification, with an indication given of how they relate to and vary with geographic context, and when exemptions would apply.
- **Sign-post policy and make the hierarchy obvious.** Ensure that users of the policy framework know where to look for different aspects of policy, and that all documents in the design policy hierarchy are fully cross-referenced.
- **Add value through control.** Development control is potentially a value-adding activity as long as enough time is made available for negotiation. Policy should encourage pre-application negotiations and clarify that sub-standard designs will be rejected.
- **Success in improving design standards takes time.** Investment is required over a sustained period of time in order to create a better local climate for delivering design quality. Do not expect immediate results.

Inset 56: Developing a planning portfolio

The ability to assess the added value provided by planning, especially development control, is limited by the lack of a tangible output. Final design ownership, in particular, is often viewed as the exclusive property of the architect, landscape architect, etc., and the role planning plays in creating high quality development is often forgotten. Planning inputs are often viewed as restrictive on design and planners find it difficult to say 'that is my work'.

The City of **Westminster** attempted to overcome this problem with their planning portfolio for design, the intention being to highlight the design value added by development control, and illustrate that planning aims to enhance the built environment not restrict innovation. The work by Westminster involved a comparative approach with original proposals juxtaposed against illustrations of final approved schemes. Before and after images highlight design improvements at the scheme and detail level, with selected schemes ranging in type and use. The comparative images also show improvements in the quality of information provided. Such documentation offers both a

sense of achievement for planning officers and enhances the public image of planning. In Westminster a dispute over one of the illustrated schemes prevented the final publication of the document, and highlights the potential difficulties of getting permission to illustrate bad practice as well as good.

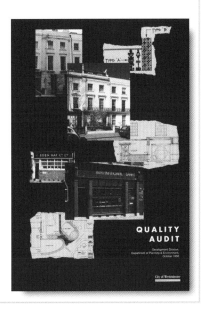

- **Councillors' backing is decisive.** Commitment and support from elected members (both in resources and in backing officer decisions) is fundamental to long-term success.

- **Fight appeals.** A good track record in winning appeals is important to policy success. The Planning Inspectorate regularly upholds appeals fought solely on design.

- **Monitoring requires investment.** Monitoring takes time and resources, but also leads to more effective policy frameworks. Monitoring can also double up as ongoing appraisal.

- **Quality review the policy framework.** Proactive reviewing of policy to ensure that all policies aim to deliver better quality more sustainable development is useful. This process can be undertaken in-house, if a suitable skill base exists, or by external advisors.

- **Set an example.** Authorities can set an example by their own actions. If the public realm is poorly cared for, and if the local authority's own developments are poorly designed, then why should private developers deliver to a higher standard?

7

Other influences on improving design quality

Other influences on improving design quality

Beyond design policy

This guidance is deliberately focused on one aspect of the design and planning agenda — writing design policies. The research on which this advice is based revealed both a strong endorsement of the importance of design policies in existing development plans, but also some scepticism across all user groups about whether such policies would fundamentally impact on the design quality of development. A number of factors were seen as impediments to improved design quality:

Inset 57: Research and the plan

Many local authorities are now investing in urban design training for staff. This investment is necessitated by the general design skills shortage and the renewed emphasis on design in planning. The standard approach is to offer part-time study opportunities on postgraduate urban design courses, an approach that helps to keep local authorities in touch with changes in urban design thinking. **Leicester** has successfully learnt from this experience with ideas explored at university subsequently being translated into design policies for the plan. Leicester's Policy UD11, for example, was born out of a thesis investigating corner buildings. **Leeds** has chosen to work with urban design students on live projects. Much of the groundwork for their 'City Centre Urban Design Strategy' was undertaken by students at Leeds Metropolitan University (see **Inset 21**). This approach benefits all concerned; students gain experience on real projects and council staff have the opportunity to keep abreast of new urban design techniques. The drive to improve local authority urban design skills is also strengthening links between academic providers and the planning department. Some planning schools provide consultant

Leicester, Design opportunities and corners

services and work with local authorities on urban design projects. This system can improve in-house urban design skills by teaching on the job, as does the retention of design consultancies to prepare various pieces of supplementary design guidance.

Leicester: UD11 Corner Buildings

3.40. Corner sites require special consideration. Their high visibility can make them important as local or major landmarks. If designed well they can increase the visual surveillance of the street, stimulate the mixing of uses and provide good enclosure of the public realm.

3.41 Larger corner plots should be incorporated into new residential development to allow for robust, adaptable, legible corner buildings. Larger plots provide greater flexibility in the size of the dwelling that can be accommodated, allow for planned expansion and provide the flexibility to accommodate other uses in the future.

UD11. CORNER BUILDINGS

The design and layout of corner buildings in new development will be expected to aid legibility, create visual interest, maximize visual surveillance and positively contribute to the vitality of the public realm by:

a) **emphasizing the importance of corners by either raising the height or profile of the corner, incorporating distinctive design materials and architectural features, accommodating different uses, providing quality planting and boundary treatment, or a combination of the above;**

b) **being located to the front of the plot and ensuring the number of principal windows overlooking the street is maximized; and,**

c) **ensuring that large blank walls or fences are avoided at the side of the property fronting onto the highway.**

In new residential development, innovative solutions to the provision of amenity space and maintaining privacy by design will be encouraged at corner sites.

Inset 58: The value of urban design

Birmingham's City Centre Urban Design Strategy (BUDS) published in 1990 is still one of the most sophisticated area appraisals undertaken in the UK. Analysis included character mapping of townscape opportunities in twelve areas, establishing clear design themes and identifying potential design opportunities. The report also provided useful guidance for development controllers with 16 key tests/questions for the development of character and the assessment of planning applications.

In 2001 the strategy still informed the deposit UDP and retained supplementary design guidance status. For example, officers highlighted their use of the sections on 'developing and protecting views' and 'reinforcing topography' when assessing proposals for new high-rise buildings. Nevertheless, the age of BUDs inevitably means that its utility is declining, with other city-wide and local guidance filling the gap (see **Inset 49**). Its success is reflected in a wide range of high quality public and private developments across Birmingham which illustrate a new local acceptance of the value of better design and the need to effectively reconnect the city centre with its surrounding neighbourhoods. Public realm improvements in Victoria and Centenary Squares, around St Philips Cathedral or along New Street provide exemplars of public realm improvements, while private developments at Brindley Place, The Mailbox, or on the site of the former Bullring Shopping Centre provide new high quality mixed use environments.

The combination of consistent and considerable investment in the public realm, and a relentless pursuit of better quality development, have to a large extent transformed national and international perceptions of Birmingham and dispelled its image as a car-dominated and uninviting place. Today Birmingham is attracting considerable private sector

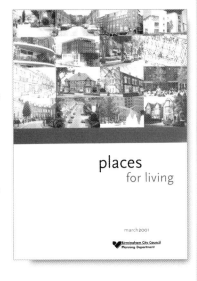

investment in the central city once again, success that is having far reaching social and economic benefits for the city, as well as environmental ones. For the authority, the challenge is now to spread this success beyond the city centre and new guidance in *Places for Living* and *Places for All* are part of this process. *Places for Living* provides residential design guidance and aims to be both inspiring and positive in encouraging quality residential proposals. The city's residential agenda is being taken forward in six main principles: places not estates, moving around easily, safe places, private spaces, building for the future, and build on local character. *Places for All* provides general design guidance for the entire city and emphasises creating diversity as an overarching theme.

To a significant extent the success story at Birmingham has been founded on: a recognition that the built environment was actively working against attempts to revive the city's economy; a need to establish a robust design vision based on an in-depth understanding of context; relentless pursuit of quality though all policy; sustained investment in the public realm; and the full use of statutory powers available to the local authority.

Birmingham, Victoria Square, before

Birmingham, Victoria Square, after

- Foremost among these were the nature of the development industry, its profit-driven motive and the lack of patronage of good design.
- Almost equal in importance were the nature of public taste, the general levels of design literacy and the conservatism (anti-modernism) of the public.
- A third key factor identified was the dearth of urban design skills in both the planning and architecture professions, but primarily on the control side (**Inset 57**).
- A fourth factor was the capabilities of councillors and the nature of local politics, particularly matters of planning gain as they affect design quality.
- A final factor focused on the lack of public sector investment in the public realm or leadership in design quality.

Therefore, although these recommendations for design policy offer the prospect of less confrontation with designers and developers, more responsiveness to place and community, and a closer focus on the fundamentals of urban and environmental design, they also represent just one part of a necessarily much broader strategy to secure better design quality. Adoption of the recommendations will however be an important step for most planning authorities and will contribute to a more enlightened and effective control regime. Nevertheless, to ensure successful implementation, the policies will still require improved officer design skills, more design awareness (particularly among councillors), and further support in guidance by central Government. Good design will also require more public sector investment in the public realm (see **Inset 38**) and the capital web and political acceptance locally of the value of good design (**Inset 58**). Most importantly, it will require an acceptance that responsibility for good design lies primarily with those who choose to develop, so requiring a greater emphasis on design quality from developers than hitherto has often been the case.

A place to start

Since the research began on which this guidance is based, the attitude of Government and many of the development professions to design — particularly urban design — has come full-circle. Thus with the publication of PPG1 in 1997, *By Design* and the Urban White Paper in 2000, and *Better Places to Live* in 2001, a very positive series of messages on design are consistently being reinforced by central Government. These are complemented by the new professional commitment to urban design inherent in the establishment of UDAL and the range of inter-professional concordats now agreed. Furthermore, recent research published in *The Value of Urban Design* has indicated that the development industries are beginning to equate the notion of design quality with enhanced economic returns. Perhaps most importantly, the changes to the planning system first mooted through the Planning Green Paper promise to put proactive planning once more at the heart of the new system.

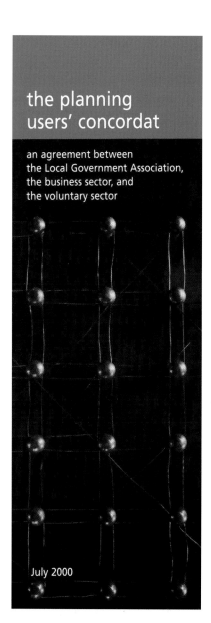

the planning users' concordat

an agreement between the Local Government Association, the business sector, and the voluntary sector

July 2000

Planning authorities have a vital role to play in delivering on this potential. A fundamental review of design policies in existing plans is the best place to start followed by their progressive incorporation into the new frameworks, plans and strategies now emerging. With the right tools in place, planners and local authorities can become the 'champions' of better design, guiding the agenda in a proactive manner, and utilising the full range of policy instruments and negotiating skills at their disposal, confident that their actions are underpinned by adopted planning policy (**Figure 5**).

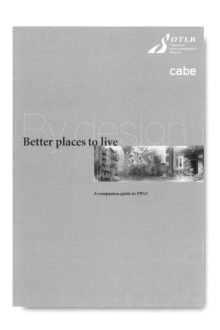

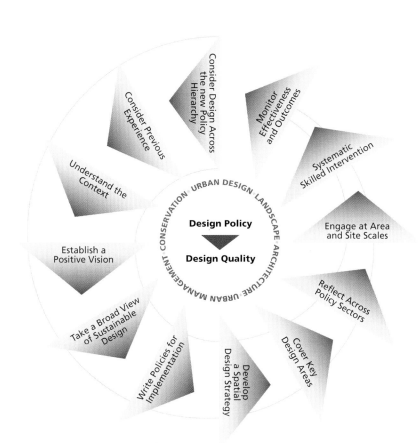

Figure 5: Key stages in design policy writing

8

References
and sources of
further advice

References and sources of further advice

Carmona, M. (2001). *Housing Design Quality, Through Policy, Guidance and Review*. Spon Press, London.

Carmona, M., de Magalhaes, C. T. and Edwards, M. (2001). *The Value of Urban Design*. Thomas Telford (for the CABE and DETR), London.

Carmona, M., Carmona, S. and Gallent, N. (2001). *Working Together, A Guide for Planners and Housing Providers*. Thomas Telford (for the RTPI, Housing Corporation, DTLR, HBF and NHF), London.

Commission for Architecture and the Built Environment (2002). *Design Review*. CABE, London.

Commission for Architecture and the Built Environment (2002). *Better Civic Buildings and Spaces*. CABE, London.

Commission for Architecture and the Built Environment and Office of the Deputy Prime Minister (2002). *Paving the Way, How we Achieve Clean, Safe and Attractive Streets*. Thomas Telford, London.

Department for the Environment, Transport and the Regions (2000). *Our Towns and Cities: The Future*. HMSO, London.

Department for the Environment, Transport and the Regions (2001). *Preparing Community Strategies, Government Guidance to Local Authorities*. DETR, London.

Department for the Environment, Transport and the Regions and Commission for Architecture and the Built Environment (2000). *By Design, Urban Design in the Planning System: Towards Better Practice*. Thomas Telford, London.

Department for Transport, Local Government and the Regions (2001). *Planning: Delivering a Fundamental Change*. DTLR, London.

Department for Transport, Local Government and the Regions and Commission for Architecture and the Built Environment (2001). *Better Places to Live, By Design*. Thomas Telford, London.

Department of the Environment (1992). *Development Plans, A Good Practice Guide*. HMSO, London.

Department of the Environment (Northern Ireland) (2000). *Creating Places, Achieving Quality in Residential Developments*. DoE (NI), Belfast.

English Heritage (1997). *Conservation Area Appraisals*. English Heritage, London.

English Heritage and Commission for Architecture and the Built Environment (2001). *Building in Context, New Development in Historic Areas*. English Heritage and CABE, London.

HM Government (2000). *Better Public Buildings, A Proud Legacy for the Future*. DCMS, London.

Institution of Civil Engineers (2002). *The 2002 Designing Streets for People Report*. ICE, London.

Layard, A., Davoudi, S. and Batty, S. (eds) (2001). *Planning for a Sustainable Future*. Spon Press, London.

Llewelyn-Davies, (2000). *Urban Design Compendium*. English Partnerships and the Housing Corporation, London.

Local Government Association (2000). *The Planning Users' Concordat, An Agreement Between the Local Government Association, the Business Sector and the Voluntary Sector*. Local Government Association, London.

Office of the Deputy Prime Minister (2002). *Sustainable Communities — Delivering through Planning*. ODPM, London.

Office of the Deputy Prime Minister (2002). *Making the System Work Better — Planning at Regional and Local Levels*. ODPM, London.

Office of the Deputy Prime Minister (2002). *Making Plans, A Practical Guide*. ODPM, London.

Planning Officers Society (1997). *Better Local Plans, A Guide to Writing Effective Policies*. POS. www.planningoffices.org.uk

Planning Officers Society (1999). *Planning and Design, Achieving Good Design Through the Planning Process*. POS. www.planning.org.uk

Planning Officers Society (1999). *Moving Towards Excellence in Urban Design and Conservation*. POS. www.planningoffices.org.uk

Punter, J., Carmona, M. and Platts, A. (1996). *Design Policies in Local Plans, A Research Report*. DoE, London.

Punter, J. and Carmona, M. (1997). *The Design Dimension of Planning, Theory, Content and Best Practice for Design Policies*. E & FN Spon, London.

Punter, J. (1999). *Design Guidelines in American Cities, A Review of Design Policies and Guidance in Five West Coast Cities*. Liverpool University Press, Liverpool.

Royal Fine Art Commission (1994). *What Makes a Good Building?* RFAC (now CABE), London.

Scottish Executive (2001). *A Policy Statement on Architecture for Scotland*. Scottish Executive, Edinburgh.

Scottish Executive (2001). *Designing Places, A Policy Statement for Scotland*. Scottish Executive, Edinburgh.

Urban Design Alliance (2001). *Arm Yourself with a Placecheck, A Users' Guide*. UDAL, London.

Urban Design Group. (2002). *Urban Design Guidance: Urban Design Frameworks, Development Briefs and Master Plans*. Thomas Telford, London.

Urban Design Skills Working Group (2001). *Urban Design Skills Working Group, Report to the Minister for Housing, Planning and Regeneration, DTLR*. CABE, London.

Urban Task Force (1999). *Towards an Urban Renaissance*. E & FN Spon, London.